Not a Madam Tussauds
the ages but an expansic
Hebrews 12:1 for us to le
was impressed on my mind as I delved in the pages of this precious book. Ten Christian leaders from Athanasius to Dietrich Bonhoeffer are introduced through the lenses of their biography and their main contributions and struggles. Each presentation ends with an interesting section on their legacy which reaches beyond their historical context, without falling into the trap of a misguided form of Protestant hagiography. The book is an excellent read to stir the passion for Church history and to encourage the development of a historical awarenness for our faith.

Leonardo De Chirico
Pastor of the church Breccia di Roma, Rome, Italy
Lecturer in Historical theology at Istituto di Formazione
Evangelica e Documentazione (Padova, Italy)
Director of the Refomanda Iniatiative

If you think church history and theology is just dead guys from the distant past saying complicated things, this book is for you. In *10 Dead Guys You Should Know* the lives, thinking and impact of ten of the most important 'dead guys' have been brought to life. Famous names become interesting characters and big ideas are explained simply and clearly in a way that shows why they are still important today.

Clare Heath-Whyte
Speaker and author of several books, including *Everyone a Child Should Know* and *First Wives' Club*

I warmly commend this page-turner, not least as an appetizer which will encourage you to delve more deeply into various aspects of Church (including missionary) history across the centuries.

Here we learn that Christian doctrine is only ever provisional and is advanced and honed often only through the fires of controversy. We learn also how God can use individuals with 'feet of clay'. ... But perhaps above all this book reminded me of how often suffering has been the lot of those whose ministry the Lord has blessed abundantly. Here we learn of Anselm who followed God's calling very much against his father's wishes; of Luther who was excommunicated; of Baxter who was ejected from his church; of Hudson Taylor, founder of the China Inland Mission, who suffered multiple bereavements on the mission field, losing his wife and three of their children, in their pursuit of the call of God on their lives; of Spurgeon, who had to cope with physical suffering as a result of severe gout, and 'struggled with depression most of his life' – suffering, which he himself described as 'the best piece of furniture I have in my house.' And, finally, there is Bonhoeffer who refused to bow the knee to Hitler and became one of the leaders of what became known as the 'Confessing Church'....

May these sketches challenge, perhaps correct, yet also motivate you to emulate significant aspects of these examples of committed, costly Christian discipleship.

Hector Morrison
Principal, Highland Theological College, UHI, Dingwall, Scotland

Challenging historical amnesia, this delightful little book presents ten Christian leaders whose legacies continue to shape our faith and practice today. Readers will learn about Athanasius' defense of the full deity of the Son of God, Augustine's insistence on grace to overcome the daunting corruption of sin, Martin Luther's heroic stand against a corrupt Roman Catholic Church, Thomas Cranmer's courageous martyrdom, and more. Each snapshot combines a brief biographical presentation with important lessons for the church to learn about obedience, faith, holiness, perseverance, courage, and mission. If readers are not familiar with these ten towering figures from the past, this book will bring them alive for today!

Gregg R. Allison
Professor of Christian Theology, The Southern Baptist
Theological Seminary, Louisville, Kentucky

This insightful collection of ten Christian leaders from different times and places reveal that knowing the past can be both liberating and illuminating. Maddock, Coulton, and Ciano ably demonstrate how earlier theologians, pastors, martyrs, and missionaries sought to live out the gospel and challenge contemporary readers to be faithful disciples of Jesus as well. This welcome introduction is well-researched, reflective, warm-hearted, and witty.

Tom Schwanda
Associate professor Emeritus, Christian Formation and Ministry,
Wheaton College, Wheaton, Illinois

10 DEAD GUYS YOU SHOULD KNOW

—

STANDING ON THE SHOULDERS OF GIANTS

EDITED BY IAN J. MADDOCK

CHRISTIAN
FOCUS

Copyright © Ian J. Maddock, Stuart Coulton & Rachel Ciano 2021

Paperback ISBN: 978-1-5271-0608-6
ePub ISBN: 978-1-5271-0681-9
Mobi ISBN: 978-1-5271-0682-6

Published in 2021
by
Christian Focus Publications Ltd,
Geanies House, Fearn, Ross-shire
IV20 1TW, Scotland
www.christianfocus.com

Cover design by Pete Barnsley

Printed and bound by
Bell & Bain, Glasgow

CONTENTS

Introduction: Two (or Ten!) Heads Are Better Than One

IAN J. MADDOCK

'I've got no creed but the Bible!' For Christians committed to the authority of the Bible, a statement like this can possess a certain allure. After all, wasn't it Peter who said to Jesus, 'Lord, to whom shall we go? You have the words of eternal life' (John 6:68, ESV)? And yet, however attractive it might sound, the reality is that none of us think or live the Christian life in a historical vacuum. While Christians have always privileged the Bible as our ultimate authority in matters of faith and practice, we've also typically recognised that the Christian life is both an intergenerational and communal activity. On the one hand, it is every generation's responsibility to embrace 'the faith that was once for all delivered' (Jude 3); none of us directly inherit the faith of those who've gone ahead of us. But, on the other hand, we also stand on the shoulders of those who've gone before us. How short-sighted it would be not to glean insights from our ancestors, whether that entails learning how to walk in their steps—or else avoiding their missteps.

One of the founding fathers of the evangelical movement in the eighteenth century, John Wesley, captured this tension. On one level, Wesley's greatest desire was to be a *homo unius libri*: a man of one book. When it came to knowing God, his first instinct was to go straight to the Bible. He wrote, 'Here then I am, far from the busy ways of men. I sit down alone: only God is here. In his presence I open, I read his Book; for this end, to find the way to heaven. Is there a doubt concerning the meaning of what I read? Does anything appear dark or intricate? I lift up my heart to the Father of lights.'[1]

But Wesley also knew from experience that reading and interpreting the Bible in splendid isolation was a recipe for theological eccentricity. He might have expressed an idealistic wish to preach as if he had 'never read one author, ancient or modern (always excepting the inspired)', but Wesley was sensitive to the dangers of unconstrained individualism, actively embracing the wisdom to be found in the writings and biographies of Christians who had long since died. And so when it came to living the Christian life, he modelled *sola* Scriptura, not *solo* Scriptura. The Bible might have been his normative authority, but not his sole authority: 'If any doubt remains,' he wrote, 'I consult those who are

---

1   A. Outler, *Sermons*; The Works of John Wesley: Bicentennial Edition 1-4 (Nashville, TN: Abingdon, 1985), 1:105-6.

experienced in the things of God, and then the writings whereby, being dead, they yet speak.'[2]

John Wesley is one of ten dead guys we, the authors of this collection of short introductory biographies, think you should know. Together they span almost the entire scope of the Church's existence and a variety of geographic locations: from Athanasius in fourth century northern Africa to Bonhoeffer in twentieth century Germany. They held a range of different opinions about how Christians ought to organise themselves and practice the sacraments; from the Anglican Thomas Cranmer to the Baptist Charles Spurgeon. They held differing positions regarding the divine-human relationship in salvation; some, like Wesley, had a lifelong allergic reaction to the idea of unconditional predestination, while others like Augustine found great comfort and assurance in this doctrine. Some, like Hudson Taylor, left his home and took the gospel to a place where it had never been heard before; others, like Martin Luther—armed with no less missionary zeal—stayed at home and proclaimed the gospel in a place where it had long been forgotten. Some, like Anselm, occupied positions of significant formal authority and influence; others, like Luther, spoke truth to ecclesiastical power despite the very real threat of censure and even death.

But for all of their differences, these dead guys shared one thing in common: not simply a passion for

---

2   Ibid.

the gospel of salvation by grace through faith in Christ alone, but a passionate zeal for preaching that gospel, even when it meant risking their personal reputations and safety. None were armchair theologians. Indeed, all of them suffered in various ways throughout their public ministries, whether the persecution took the form of multiple exiles (Athanasius), being ejected from one's church and being imprisoned (Richard Baxter), or ultimately, martyrdom (Cranmer).

Appreciating the past doesn't always come naturally for us living in the twenty-first century. The world we live in often equates newer with better and older with obsolete. If the young are our future, then the old are 'over the hill.' In an environment such as this that (wittingly or otherwise) encourages historical amnesia, we aren't conditioned to intuitively see value in the past. 'Not, of course, that there is any magic about the past,' suggests C. S. Lewis. 'People were no cleverer then than they are now; they made as many mistakes as we. But not the same mistakes. They will not flatter us in the errors we are already committing; and their own errors, being now open and palpable, will not endanger us.' His conclusion? 'Two heads are better than one, not because either is infallible, but because they are unlikely to go wrong in the same direction.'[3]

We think Lewis was on to something profoundly insightful. And if it's indeed true that two heads are

---

3 C. S. Lewis, Introduction to *On the Incarnation* by Athanasius (Crestwood, N.Y.: SVS, 1998), pp. 4-5.

better than one, then how much more ten! These chapters emerge from the experience Stuart Coulton, Rachel Ciano and I have had teaching Church History together at Sydney Missionary and Bible College, Australia's oldest interdenominational seminary. It's been our privilege to introduce many cohorts of undergraduate and graduate students to the wealth of benefit and joy that comes with studying the way God has sustained His Church throughout time and space, and we're thankful now for the opportunity to share our passion with a wider audience through this book.

Athanasius
Against the World

Stuart Coulton

Tyre is a city built on a rocky outcrop jutting into the Mediterranean Sea in what is modern day Lebanon. It was here in A.D. 335 that the Bishop of Alexandria was summoned by the Roman Emperor Constantine to appear before a gathering of fellow bishops and answer charges that had been brought against him. Athanasius was at the centre of a theological storm surrounding the Church's understanding of Jesus. For well over a decade debate had raged as to whether Jesus was in some way or other created by God, or was in fact eternally of the same essence as God.

But Athanasius was being called before the gathering of bishops, not to debate the divinity of Jesus, but to answer the charge that he had murdered a man—Arsenius—cut off his arm and used that arm in the practice of sorcery! It was an accusation that had surfaced earlier but had been answered to the Emperor's satisfaction. Now it had resurfaced and Athanasius interpreted the accusation as being yet another salvo fired off by those who opposed him in the theological debate over Jesus.

Athanasius' accusers produced, to the watching church leaders at the Council of Tyre, a hand which they claimed was that removed by Athanasius from the man he had murdered. In what must have been a wonderful piece of theatre, Athanasius then produced a live Arsenius to the Synod of bishops! The accusation of murder having been readily dismissed, there was still the matter of the missing hand. Athanasius had Arsenius dramatically led into the chamber with both his hands concealed by a cloak. In front of the watching bishops Athanasius first revealed one hand to the gathering, paused for effect, then exhibited Arsenius' second hand which was also still attached to his body. Athanasius then addressed the gathering:

> Arsenius, as you see, is found to have two hands: let my accusers show the place whence the third was cut off.[1]

The event was typical of the world of swirling accusation and counter accusation, intrigue and plotting that characterised the Church's debate over this important

---

1   Socrates, *The Eccclesiastical History* 1.29 (*NPNF*[2] Vol. 2, p. 31). See also Sozomen, *The Ecclesiastical History* 2.25 (*NPNF*[2] Vol. 2, p. 275) and Athanasius, *Defence Against the Arians* 6.72 (*NPNF*[2] Vol. 4, p. 137–38). *NPNF*[2] is the *Nicene and Post-Nicene Fathers*, Second Series. Edited by Philip Schaff and Henry Wace. 14 vols. Repr. Grand Rapids, MI: Eerdmans, 1978.

theological issue. And Athanasius was always at its centre!

Formative Years

Athanasius was born into a vital hub of Christianity—Alexandria, Egypt—sometime in the closing days of the third century. Uncertainty over the year of his birth actually proved to be important—one of the many accusations leveled against him was that he was under the legal age for a bishop when he was installed as Bishop of Alexandria in 328.[2] Whilst not a great deal is known about his early years, it is clear that Athanasius at a fairly young age was taken under the wing, educated and prepared for a life of service in the Church, by the Bishop of Alexandria at the time—a man confusingly named Alexander.

By the time Athanasius had reached his late teens, he had already lived through such a terrible period of persecution of Christians that it came to be known as the *Great Persecution*,[3] and the equally turbulent events surrounding the conversion to Christianity of Constantine,[4] who would eventually by force of arms establish himself as sole Emperor of the Roman Empire.

---

2 Athanasius, *Festal Letters and Their Index: Index* 3. (*NPNF²* Vol. 4, p.503). See also Khaled Anatolios, *Athanasius*, (The Early Church Fathers; London: Routledge, 2004), p. 5.

3 Roman Emperor Diocletian began the persecution in 303.

4 For details of Constantine's conversion, see Sozomen, Ecclesiastical History, III (*NPNF²* Vol. 2, p. 283ff).

The advent of a Christian emperor coincided with a period of great theological controversy, as the Church wrestled with its understanding of the nature of the Lord Jesus Christ.

On the Incarnation

The controversy began in Alexandria when a presbyter (that is, a pastor or elder) called Arius challenged Bishop Alexander's understanding of the relationship between Jesus and God. Whilst there are various versions of events, what is clear is that Arius accused Alexander of holding to a heresy that blended the Father, Son and Spirit so closely as to lose their distinctiveness.[5] Very little of what Arius actually wrote has survived to us today. His main theological work was called the *Thalia*. Interestingly, it was written in verse, and a form of verse that at the time was more commonly associated with popular and often bawdy songs.[6] An unorthodox, but effective, way to spread his views! The little that survives of the *Thalia* comes to us courtesy of Athanasius. So there is naturally a degree of scepticism about how accurately Athanasius represented Arius' opinions. However, even the most sceptical are inclined to accept as authentic a passage from the *Thalia* which Athanasius reproduces:

---

5   The heresy was called Sabellianism.

6   R.P.C. Hanson, *The Search for the Christian Doctrine of God* (Edinburgh: T & T Clark, 1988), p. 10.

> The Unbegun made the Son ... For He is not equal, no,
> nor one in essence with Him ... Foreign from the Son
> in essence is the Father, for He is without beginning ...
> though the Son was not, the Father was God.[7]

This passage is consistent with the way Athanasius
presents Arius' position elsewhere in his writings. Arius
set forth a view of Jesus as God's Son that separated
Him from God the Father. Arius argued that since Jesus
was the Son of God, there must have been a point when
He became the Son. Therefore Jesus was not eternal; at
some point He had not existed:

> God was not always a Father: The Son was not always
> .... And since all things are creatures, He also is a
> creature and a thing made ... there was a time when
> the Word of God Himself was not.[8]

Arius goes on to insist that Jesus did not share God's
essence. That which makes God to be God was not
present in Jesus. This issue of essence—expressed in the
Greek word *ousia*—lay at the heart of the debate. It
was clearly an issue of tremendous importance for the
Church. How could Jesus be worshiped as God if He
did not share in the very essence of God but was in fact

---

7   Athanasius, *Councils of Ariminum and Seleucia* 2.15 (*NPNF*[2]
    Vol. 4, p. 457). For a helpful discussion of this issue see Hanson,
    Search, pp. 5-15.

8   Athanasius, *To the Bishops of Egypt* 2.12 (*NPNF*[2] Vol. 4, p. 229).
    See also Socrates, *Ecclesiastical History*, I.5 (*NPNF*[2] Vol. 2, p. 3).

a part of the creation? How could Jesus save unless He was not only human but also divine?[9] Can we know God through Jesus if Jesus is not Himself God? Athanasius rightly observed that Arius was teaching that:

> ... the Son can neither see nor know the Father perfectly and exactly. For having a beginning of existence, He [Jesus] cannot know Him [God the Father] that is without beginning...[10]

So far as Athanasius was concerned, the teaching of Arius threatened everything the Bible had to say about salvation.[11] So he wrote:

> ...to change the corruptible to incorruption was proper to none other than the Saviour Himself, who in the beginning made all things out of nothing; that only the Image of the Father could re-create the likeness of the Image in men, that none save our Lord Jesus Christ could give to mortals immortality, and that only the Word Who ... is alone the Father's true and sole-begotten Son could teach men about Him...[12]

---

9   David M. Gwyn, *Athanasius of Alexandria: Bishop, Theologian, Ascetic, Father* (Christian Theology in Context. Oxford: OUP, 2012), p. 70.

10 Athanasius, *To the Bishops of Egypt* 2.12 (*NPNF*[2] Vol. 4, p. 229).

11 Gwyn, *Athanasius*, p. 80.

12 Athanasius, *On the Incarnation* 4.19 (London: A.R. Mowbray & Co, 1953).

Athanasius goes on to argue that 'having proved his Godhead by his works', Jesus was then in a position where He could 'offer the sacrifice on behalf of all.' [13]

Arius' views began to win significant support all around the Mediterranean, prompting Alexander to call a meeting of church leaders from across North Africa, who agreed to condemn Arius' teaching as heretical and excommunicate him.[14] But Arius had managed to win over some influential supporters, none more so than Eusebius, the Bishop of Nicomedia (modern day Izmit, Turkey) who strenuously advocated for Arius' restoration.[15] By the time Emperor Constantine had established himself as sole ruler of the Roman Empire, it was an Empire shattered by theological disharmony! Recognising that a united Christianity was necessary to help hold together his vast, sprawling and diverse Empire, Constantine called together the leaders of the Church to a Council in Nicaea (modern day Iznik, Turkey).[16]

They met in May 325 with the Emperor himself attending at key points. It is difficult to know exactly how many people attended—probably over 300 bishops

---

13 Ibid.

14 Socrates, *Ecclesiastical History*, I.6 (*NPNF²* Vol. 2, pp. 3–6).

15 Athanasius, *Against the Arians*, 6 (*NPNF²* Vol. 4, pp. 137–47). Socrates, *Ecclesiastical History*, I.6 (*NPNF²* Vol. 2, pp. 3–6).

16 An Ecumenical Council referred to the fact that the whole Church was meant to be involved—up to this point various councils had been regional in character. The Council of Nicaea is recognised as the first of seven such councils in the history of the early Church.

and numerous support staff as well. The likelihood of a consensus seemed remote at the start. Many of the church leaders attending brought written complaints about each other, hoping to gain the ear of the emperor. However, Constantine opened proceedings by burning all the pleadings handed him![17]

The outcome of the Council was a resounding defeat for Arius and his supporters. Much of the debate centred around whether it was correct to speak of the Son being of the *same* essence (Greek—*homo-ousios*) as the Father, or of *similar* essence (*homoi-ousios*). In Greek the difference was one letter, but the difference in meaning for how we are to understand who Jesus is was enormous. The Council decided in favour of *homo-ousios* (same essence) and issued a creedal statement[18] expressing a view of Jesus which preserved the biblical doctrine of His divinity, stating categorically that Jesus was:

> ...of the substance of the Father ... consubstantial [homo-ousios] with the Father.[19]

---

17 Socrates, *Ecclesiastical History* 1.8 (*NPNF²* Vol. 2, pp. 8–12). See also Sozomen, *Ecclesiastical History* 1.17 (*NPNF²* Vol. 2, p. 253).

18 This statement by the Council of Nicaea was adapted in 381 at the Council of Constantinople, and that adapted creedal statement is what today we call the Nicene Creed.

19 Socrates, *Ecclesiastical History* 1.8. (*NPNF²* Vol. 2, p. 10).

Athanasius Contra Mundum[20]

Sadly, that was not the end of the matter. By the time Alexander died in 328, the debate was still raging and Arius and his supporters were making strong headway. Alexander was succeeded by his young protégé, Athanasius. Athanasius' ministry was to be one long controversy which began with his election as Bishop. He was opposed not only by supporters of Arius, but by a breakaway group within the North African Church known as the Melitians, who had severed ties with the mainstream Church over issues of church discipline. It was alleged that Athanasius had not been elected according to due process[21] and was too young to have been elected Bishop being still under thirty.[22]

Athanasius' election, however, stood. One of his first challenges was to deal with a forceful demand from Eusebius of Nicomedia to reinstate Arius to fellowship. Eusebius had been vigorously lobbying the Emperor, arguing that to exclude Arius from the Church was to persist in a harmful division.[23] He also raised a variety of serious allegations against Athanasius. The allegations didn't relate to the theological differences that existed—Athanasius was a staunch defender of the outcome of the Council of Nicaea, so no traction

---

20 'Against the world.'

21 Athanasius, *Against the Arians* 1.6 (*NPNF²* Vol. 4, pp. 103–4).

22 Hanson, *Search*, p. 247.

23 Athanasius, *Against the Arians* 5.59 (*NPNF²* Vol. 4, pp. 131–2).

could be gained on that front. However, Athanasius was accused of imposing a tax on linen products, inciting violence against the Melitians by encouraging one of his presbyters, Macarius, to smash a cup used in celebration of the Lord's supper, and 'being an enemy of the Emperor.'[24] These were charges that when Athanasius met with Constantine in person he was able to refute to the Emperor's satisfaction. It was then that the accusations regarding Arsenius began to surface.[25]

At the Council of Tyre in 335, despite the dramatic exposure by Athanasius of the attempt to frame him for murder, things went badly for the Alexandrian Bishop. The accusation regarding the murder of Arsenius was one of many charges of violence leveled against him.[26] Realising that he had no chance of avoiding censure at the Council (which did condemn Athanasius, deposed him as Bishop of Alexandria and exiled him from the city), Athanasius hurriedly sailed in an open boat[27] to Constantinople where he rushed up to the Emperor in the middle of the road as Constantine rode with his entourage. It was an unorthodox way to seek an audience with the Emperor—and it almost backfired. A clearly annoyed Emperor's first reaction was to ride on

---

24 Athanasius, *Against the Arians* 5.60 (*NPNF*[2] Vol. 4, p.132). See also Sozomen, *Ecclesiastical History* 2.22 (*NPNF*[2] Vol. 2, pp. 272–3).

25 Ibid., 5.63 (*NPNF*[2] Vol. 4, p. 133).

26 Sozomen, *Ecclesiastical History* 2.25 (*NPNF*[2] Vol. 2, pp. 275–6).

27 Athanasius, *Festal Letters and Their Index: Index* 8. (*NPNF*[2] Vol. 4, p. 503).

and have this nuisance removed. However, Athanasius persisted and eventually won, not an audience with Constantine, but at least agreement to his demand that his accusers from the Council of Tyre be summoned to Constantinople.[28] Athanasius was never one to stand back or leave matters to work out as they may. He took decisive action when required, always driven by a strong sense of the rightness of his cause.

Unfortunately for Athanasius, his plan did not go well. Eusebius and other leaders arrived fresh from Tyre and managed to turn the Emperor away from Athanasius with a new accusation—that the Bishop had threatened to prevent the supply of corn being transferred from Alexandria to Constantinople. Constantine ordered Athanasius into exile immediately (335), from which he would only return on Constantine's death two years later.[29] Despite Athanasius later trying to put the best spin on it that he could—Constantine exiled him to protect him from his enemies[30]—the exile was a serious blow to the young bishop.

Following Athanasius' exile, Arius was admitted back into fellowship with the Church—by order of the Emperor. Arius had managed to convince Constantine that he held to the orthodoxy of Nicaea. According to Socrates, Constantine was surprised by the ease with which Arius was prepared to sign off on the creed of Nicaea. So

---

28 Athanasius, *Against the Arians* 6.86 (*NPNF²* Vol. 4, p. 145).

29 Ibid., 6.87 (*NPNF²* Vol. 4, p. 146).

30 Athanasius, *History of the Arians* 8.50 (*NPNF²* Vol. 4, p. 288).

he insisted Arius swear to his beliefs by an oath. Arius wrote his own beliefs out on a piece of paper, and with that paper securely under his arm, happily 'swore truly that he really *held* [my emphasis] the sentiments he had written.'[31] Socrates does admit that the story is merely hearsay—but, perhaps more accurately, skullduggery!

Arius did not live long enough to enjoy his triumphant restoration. According to Athanasius, Bishop Alexander of Constantinople (an opponent of Arius) was commanded by the Emperor to allow Arius to participate in the Lord's Supper. Distressed by this command the Bishop retired to the Church of St Irene to pray that God would remove either Arius or himself! Whilst out in the streets of Constantinople, Arius suddenly needed to go to the public latrine, and whilst inside he died. Thus an unsympathetic Athanasius tartly observed, he 'was deprived both of communion and of his life together.'[32]

The death of Arius changed nothing. In many ways he had already become irrelevant. Eusebius, Bishop of Nicomedia and a confidante of the Emperor, had taken leadership of a movement which did not even hold strictly to Arius' theology. In fact, over the coming years there would be any number of different propositions advanced as to the relationship between Jesus and God. What all would hold in common was a rejection of

---

31 Socrates, Ecclesiastical History 1.39 (*NPNF²* Vol. 2, p. 35).

32 Athanasius, *To Serapion, concerning the death of Arius*, Letter 54 (*NPNF²* Vol. 4, pp. 564–66). For an argument against the historical details of Athanasius' account see Hanson, p. 265.

the creedal statement that had been settled upon at the Council of Nicaea. They would refuse to acknowledge Jesus as the One who is God in every way, sharing in the very essence—*ousia*—of God the Father. The title *Arianism* was simply a useful way to refer to this diverse group of adherents to any unorthodox understanding of the Son which in some form or other undermined the divinity of the Son.[33] Another title often given them was that of *Eusebians*, after Arius' great supporter, Bishop Eusebius of Nicomedia.

Upon Constantine's death in 337 he was succeeded by his three rather unimaginatively named sons: Constantine, Constans and Constantius. After the early death of Constantine II, Constantius was left to rule the Eastern portion of the Empire and Constans the Western. The new regime enabled the return of Athanasius from exile. He arrived back in Alexandria to great acclaim, having called on the Eastern Emperor Constantius on his way. This was a politically astute goodwill gesture, Constantius being sympathetic to Athanasius' opponents.

However, it would not be enough to prevent a growing divide between the two sides of the Empire. Whilst generalisations inevitably don't do justice, Constans' support for Athanasius was mirrored in Athanasius' popularity with the western bishops, including Julius the Bishop of Rome. And Constantius' support for the anti-Nicaean party reflected the hostility to Athanasius

---

33 Gwyn, *Athanasius*, p. 80.

in the eastern region of the Empire. When Athanasius was exiled a second time, his replacement—Gregory of Cappadocia—arrived in Alexandria in 339 backed by the military force of the Roman prefect. This proved a necessary precaution as the city erupted in rioting!

In 346 a meeting took place between Athanasius and the Arian–leaning Emperor Constantius.[34] The meeting went well—Athanasius reported that the Emperor 'received me kindly'[35] and Athanasius was allowed to return as Bishop of Alexandria later that year.

The next decade was a good one for Athanasius. No exiles! However, the death of Constans in 350 removed from the scene a powerful ally of Athanasius' and it would be only a matter of time before the storm clouds would once again gather over Alexandria.

In February 356 Imperial forces surrounded the Alexandrian church where Athanasius was leading worship with his congregation, seeking to arrest him. In the confusion, Athanasius was able to be smuggled out in the crush of monks and clergy and went into hiding.[36] His third exile had begun.

Although Imperial forces hunted high and low for him, such was Athanasius' enormous popularity within Egypt that everywhere he went whilst in hiding he was given protection.[37] It is a testament to the pastoral investment

---

34 Anatolios, *Athanasius*, pp. 22–3.

35 Athanasius, *Against the Arians* 4.55 (*NPNF*[2] Vol. 4, pp. 129–30).

36 Athanasius, *Defence of his Flight* 24 (*NPNF*[2] Vol. 4, pp. 263–4).

37 A. Robertson, 'Prolegomena,' 2.8 (*NPNF*[2] Vol. 4, p. li).

of Athanasius during the decade he had been allowed to remain as bishop that he was so widely respected.[38]

Under intense Imperial pressure the Western bishops who had provided Athanasius with such strong support began to cave in. The Western bishops eventually signed off on a Creed which not only failed to affirm that the Father and Son were of the same essence (*homo-ousios*), but simply asserted that they were *like*—without clarifying in what ways they were, and in what ways they were not! On the last day of 359 the Eastern bishops also signed off on the Creed and it became the official creed of the whole Church.[39] The cantankerous old monk Jerome famously wrote that,

> Faith stood condemned by acclamation. The whole world groaned, and was astonished to find itself Arian.[40]

Jerome's pessimism proved to be unfounded. The battle was still not over! The death of Emperor Constantius in 360 was to not only remove a strong opponent of the outcome of the Council of Nicaea, but ushered in a new Emperor committed to restoring Paganism to the Roman Empire—Julian the Apostate. For Julian, division within the Church was to be encouraged, so following the

---

38 See Gwyn, *Athanasius*, p. 44.

39 Anatolios, *Athanasius*, pp. 29–30. See also Frend, *Early Church*, p. 168.

40 Jerome, *The Dialogue Against the Luciferians*, 19 (*NPNF*² Vol. 6, p. 329).

brutal death of Bishop George he allowed Athanasius to return from exile in 362. This didn't work out as Julian had hoped. Athanasius' huge influence meant that Christianity prospered under his ministry, and later that year he was back in exile for the fourth time![41]

Julian's attempt to take Rome back to the worship of the old pagan gods proved futile. His death in 363 brought another Christian Emperor to the throne—Jovian—and Athanasius returned to Alexandria. Jovian's death in 364, however, brought to power Valentinian and his anti-Nicene brother Valens. In 365 Imperial troops again besieged the church where Athanasius was worshiping in an attempt to capture him, but again the wily bishop escaped—into his fifth and final exile. Despite his dislike of Athanasius, Valens' tenuous political position in Egypt prompted him to restore the influential bishop to Alexandria[42] in 366, where he was to remain until his death in 373.

Despite the political turmoil, the theological tide had turned. Increasingly those opposed to the Nicene Creed were becoming marginalised and many who had previously been opponents of the Nicene Creed had begun to come around—motivated perhaps by a fear of the very radical doctrines being pushed by some.[43] It is this diversity within the anti-Nicene camp

---

41 Anatolios, *Athanasius*, pp. 31–2.

42 Anatolios, *Athanasius*, p. 32.

43 Frend, *Early Church*, p. 183.

which makes it difficult at times to clearly describe, and which contained the seeds ultimately for its failure. Some argued for *homoi-ousion* (*similar* essence), others for *homoian* (*like*, but no mention of essence) and still others for what was termed *anomian* (meaning *unlike*). Athanasius by contrast was resolute and consistent in advocating the *homo-ousion* (*same* essence) position throughout the long years of controversy.

Athanasius continued to write extensively on Christology, a highly respected figure in both the East and the West,[44] his mature reflections providing much of the foundation for future Church Councils.[45] And onto the scene came a new generation of theologians, led by Basil of Caesarea who would hold steadfastly to the Nicene Creed and succeed in formulating it in such a way that it would be given new, and final, expression at a Council held in Chalcedon in 481.

Athanasius' legacy

Athanasius was a divisive figure in his own time, and continues to divide opinion today. In recent decades his reputation has taken something of a thrashing. In his lifetime there were numerous accusations of violence leveled at Athanasius by his enemies. He was alleged to have imprisoned, flogged and tortured his opponents,[46]

---

44 Gwyn, *Athanasius*, pp. 52–3.

45 Anatolios, *Athanasius*, p. 33.

46 See Gwyn, Athanasius, pp. 28–9, 36.

and to have violently destroyed their church property.[47] He was accused of treasonously conspiring with the usurper Magnentius (who had killed Emperor Constans in 350)[48] and doing little to restrain the violence of his supporters.[49]

All of which has formed the basis for Athanasius being condemned today as a gangster who controlled an 'ecclesiastical mafia',[50] 'exercised power and protected his position in Alexandria by the systematic use of violence and intimidation',[51] 'a violent man',[52] and even 'a modern Iranian ayatollah'![53]

What sense can we make of this? Athanasius was at the centre of a controversy with accusation and counter accusation being flung back and forth. His language could on occasions be extreme, and his portrayal of those opposed to him was often an attack not only on their theology but also on their character. So it is no surprise that Athanasius' opponents should attack him personally—it was the unfortunate way in which debate

47 Athanasius, *Against the Arians* 1.11 (*NPNF*[2] Vol. 4, pp. 106–7).

48 Athanasius, *Defence Before Constantius* 6–9 (*NPNF*[2] Vol. 4, pp. 240–1).

49 Anatolios, *Athanasius*, p. 36.

50 T.D. Barnes, *Constantine and Eusebius* (Cambridge, MA: Harvard University Press; 1981), p. 230.

51 T.D. Barnes, *Athanasius and Constantius: Theology and Politics in the Constantinian Empire* (Massachusetts: Harvard University Press; 2001), p. 32.

52 P. Johnson, *A History of Christianity* (London: Penguin, 1976), p. 87.

53 David Brakke, 'Athanasius', in *The Early Christian World Volume 2*, ed. Philip F. Esler (Oxford: Routledge, 2000), p. 1109.

was conducted. Of the vast range of accusations leveled against Athanasius, a number of them were clearly false—as the story of Arsenius illustrates. And of the remainder there is no conclusive proof that Athanasius was guilty of any of the charges leveled against him.

Any assessment of Athanasius' character and actions, however, cannot be separated from the polemical context in which he lived. He was certainly dogmatic. The phrase 'Athanasius against the world' was coined with a high measure of truth to it. Athanasius needed to be dogmatic because the truth he was defending was so important. Athanasius rightly recognised that Christianity rose or fell on the Lord Jesus Christ. To deny His full divinity was to jeopardise Christian worship and the gospel of salvation itself. To the Emperor Constantine, as also to many modern ears, the matters being argued about appeared to be a case of theological hair-splitting. After all, the difference between the *homo-ousion* party and those advocating *homoi-ousion* was one letter of the Greek alphabet! Is that an argument worth having?

Athanasius' answer was a resounding *Yes!* Anything less than a biblical understanding of the divinity of Jesus was a denial of everything that was fundamental and unique to Christianity. The fact that the error of some was grammatically minor simply illustrated the point of Jerome—that many opponents of Athanasius held opinions that were like honey mixed with poison,[54] apparently sweet to the taste but deadly nonetheless.

Holding dogmatically to one truth can at times be interpreted as arrogance. Holding doggedly to what we believe to be true can make us appear to lack gentleness. Whilst gentleness and humility are essential when Christians debate and disagree over important matters, there are some truths which can nonetheless never be compromised. They are matters of first importance. And the Church needs men and women of strong character to defend those truths, who are prepared to suffer, to be maligned, and even to be ostracised for the sake of holding fast to the faith. As Paul encouraged his timid young friend Timothy:

> Guard the good deposit that was entrusted to you (2 Tim. 1:14, NIV).

We must preserve the fundamental truths of the gospel with gentleness and kindness, but with firm conviction also. Athanasius never wavered from the truth he defended. Nor must we.

For further reading:

Beckwith, Carl. 'Athanasius.' Pages 153–189 in *Shapers of Christian Orthodoxy*. Edited by Bradley Green (Nottingham: Apollos; 2010).

---

54 Jerome, *Against the Luciferians*, 17 (*NPNF*[2] Vol. 6, p. 328).

For the adventurous:

Anatolios, Khaled. *Athanasius*. The Early Church Fathers (London: Routledge, 2004).

Gwyn, David M. *Athanasius of Alexandria: Bishop, Theologian, Ascetic, Father.* Christian Theology in Context (Oxford: OUP, 2012).

Augustine
The Grace of God Defeated Me

RACHEL CIANO

A taste of Augustine

The humble pear is usually reserved for mushed baby
food, decorative food bowls, or at their most elegant,
still life paintings. But for Augustine, pears were the
substance of momentous personal regret that would
set him on a trajectory towards becoming one of the
most influential theologians in the life of the Church.
As a boy, probably as a teenager, he and his friends
used to run about town mucking about and generally
looking for trouble. One evening while out on one of
their adventures, they spotted a pear tree full of fruit.
Augustine tells us that they didn't want to eat them as
they weren't hungry and, besides, they had better ones
at home. Nevertheless, they shook the tree so the pears
would fall, and they collected up a huge score of them.
What were they going to do with a massive load of

pears they didn't want to eat? They went off to throw them at pigs, of course.

Augustine reflected a lot on his life, especially on his younger years when he wasn't a Christian, and why he did the things he did. When he later considered that night he stole pears with his friends, he grieved. He kept bringing it up and mulling it over. He wrote years later that he enjoyed stealing them just for the act itself. He loved his rebellion and took great pleasure in doing what wasn't allowed, especially with his friends. He wrote: 'The pleasure I got was not from the pears; it was in the crime itself, enhanced by the companionship of my fellow sinners…why did I find such delight in doing this which I would not have done alone? … Behold, my God, the lively review of my soul's career is laid bare before you. I would not have committed that theft alone…when they say, "Let's go, let's do it," we are ashamed not to be shameless.'[1]

Augustine's now famous book, *Confessions*, tells this story of adolescent rebellion and his sorrow over it. *Confessions* is part autobiography, part theological treatise, part prayer, and full of references to the Psalms. He published it in A.D. 397 when he was 43 years old. It is largely one long story of his conversion, of how he ran from God, and how God pursued him, wooing Augustine with his grace and love. He summed up his experience (and ours) in the preface: 'Our hearts

---

1   *Confessions*, 2:8-9 (Peabody, MA: Hendrickson Publishers, 2004), p. 35.

are restless until they find their rest in you.' Augustine was intensely aware of his sin, and consequently a great sense of God's grace towards him in forgiving him. These two truths—Augustine's right assessment of himself as a sinner, and his right assessment of God's grace towards him in his sin—are two truths that are arguably his greatest legacy to the Church. We too need constant reminders of these two foundational truths. It is Augustine's long and often fractious debate with the British theologian-monk Pelagius that led him to write about God's grace so clearly and thoughtfully. R.C. Sproul reflects: 'What would Luther think of the modern day heirs of the Reformation? My guess is that he would write on the modern church's captivity to Pelagianism.'[2] We need to hear afresh today about Augustine and what he would have the Church know about God's grace if we are to avoid the ever-present danger of Pelagianism.

God's pursuit of Augustine

Augustine led a colourful life. He was born in 354 in the North African part of the Roman Empire, which was generally considered a backwater place by those educated Romans across the Mediterranean in Italy. However, it was clear early on that he was destined

---

2   R.C. Sproul, *Willing to Believe: The Controversy over Free Will* (Grand Rapids, MI: Baker Books, 1997), p. 21. He writes this statement to say that the Church today tends to view humanity as basically good.

for greatness. While not from an overly wealthy family, they had enough connections to ensure Augustine could get a decent education that would set the family on the path of success. His stern, non-Christian father, Patricius, arranged for Augustine to leave their home in Thagaste (known today as the Algerian town of Souk Ahras) to attend university in Carthage about 300 kilometres away (in modern day Tunisia). There, he studied and later taught rhetoric. Augustine was an excellent student—curious and intelligent. He also had a way with words and a capacity for hard work, all of which meant that typically whatever he applied his hand to he did well in. Following his conversion, God would use Augustine's formidable intellect and prodigious gifting in great ways to serve the Church.

In his *Confessions* Augustine writes of sin that beset his life as a young man. *Confessions* is both an autobiographical and theological defense of original sin, which is why he devoted so much space to rehearsing the thoroughgoing pervasiveness of his sin. He wrote that when he was sixteen, 'I surrendered myself entirely to lust, which your law forbids but human hearts are not ashamed to sanction. My family made no effort to save me...their only concern was that I should learn how to make a good speech and how to persuade others by my words.'[3] He lived with a woman as his concubine for nearly fourteen years, which gave her some rights,

---

3   *Confessions*, 2:2 (London: Penguin Books, 1961), p. 44.

but they certainly weren't married, probably because Augustine's parents thought her too below him in status. They had a son together, named Adeodatus ('gift of God'), however Augustine never named this woman, perhaps because it was all too painful when it ended.

His mother, Monica, who was a devout Christian, urged Augustine to finally get married, but to someone else. A young girl from a rich family in Milan was picked out for Augustine. He had to wait two years to marry her as she was underage, and in the meantime he had to send away the mother of his child. He wrote openly of the heartache: 'The woman with whom I had been living was torn from my side as an obstacle to my marriage and this was a blow which crushed my heart to bleeding, because I loved her dearly.'[4] He could not wait for another two years, so took a mistress, and wrote, 'That wound of mine was not healed…it began to fester.'[5] 'I exhausted myself in depravity…intent on withdrawing still further from you. I loved my own way, not yours, but it was a truant's freedom that I loved.'[6] He prayed, 'give me chastity and self-control, but not yet. For I was afraid that you would answer my prayer at once and cure me too soon of the disease of lust.'[7]

---

4   *Confessions*, 6:15 (London: Penguin Books, 1961), p. 131.

5   *Confessions*, 6:15. William Harmless, *Augustine in His Own Words* (Washington, D.C.: Catholic University of America, 2010), p. 18.

6   *Confessions*, 3:3 (London: Penguin Books, 1961), pp. 57–8.

7   *Confessions*, 8:7 (London: Penguin Books, 1961), p. 169.

However, despite revelling in sin, Augustine recognised that, 'however great my indulgence in sensual pleasure, I could not find happiness.'[8]

Along the way, Augustine not only had relationships with numerous women, he also flirted with a variety of philosophical worldviews. He tried out Neo-Platonism (with its focus on the journey to the 'One'), but quickly moved on. He found a temporary, band-aid rationalization of his sin in the Manicheans. They were a heretical group who taught that there was an unbridgeable divide between the spiritual and physical world. They believed the physical world was evil and corrupted, while the spiritual world was pure and good. It was on this theological foundation that Augustine felt he could sin with his body without corrupting his spirit. No wonder he was still in such misery! Because God in the Old Testament had made the physical world, the Manicheans rejected the Old Testament. He eventually became disillusioned with the Manicheans, especially because they didn't have adequate answers for his questions regarding evil, and in time would become one of its most vocal critics.

Having rejected the Manicheans' convenient justification for continuing to sin with impunity, Augustine renewed his struggle for personal holiness, not just in the realm of lust but also when it came to personal ambition. In 384 he travelled to Milan, accepting a position as Professor of Rhetoric. It was one of the highest academic

---

8   *Confessions*, 6:16 (London: Penguin Books, 1961), p. 132.

positions in the Roman Empire, which included writing speeches for the Roman Emperor. But Milan held a more important role for Augustine than his stellar career—it was to be the place of his conversion at thirty-two years of age. This was to be the great transformation and turning point of his life. The Bishop of Milan, Ambrose, was from all accounts a compelling preacher. Augustine went along to hear Ambrose, initially just to glean some rhetorical strategies. Ambrose preached on the Old Testament, which was thrown out by the Manicheans. Hearing Ambrose preach, Augustine started to change his thinking about God. Things came to a head, and in turmoil about his life, sin and who God was, Augustine became deeply distressed to the point of tears. He went into a garden to weep alone:

> I flung myself down beneath a fig tree and gave way to the tears which now streamed from my eyes ... For I felt that I was still the captive of my sins, and in my misery I kept crying 'How long shall I go on saying "tomorrow, tomorrow"? Why not now? Why not make an end of my ugly sins at this moment?' I was asking myself these questions, weeping all the while with the most bitter sorrow in my heart, when all at once I heard the singsong voice of boy or girl ... it repeated the refrain 'take it and read.'[9]

Augustine took this as God telling him to get a Bible and read the first passage his eyes fell upon, which was

---

9   *Confessions*, 8:12 (London: Penguin Books, 1961), p. 177.

Romans 13:13. It is an appeal to holy living: 'Let us behave decently, as in the daytime, not in carousing and drunkenness, not in sexual immorality and debauchery, not in dissension and jealousy' (NIV). This clinched it for Augustine. 'In an instant, as I came to the end of the sentence, it was as though the light of confidence flooded into my heart and all the darkness of doubt was dispelled.'[10]

Augustine wrote in his *Confessions* a poetic prayer devoted to God's gracious pursuit of him:

> Late have I loved You,
> beauty so ancient,
> so new,
> late have I loved You.
>
> And see; You were within, inside me,
> and I was outside,
> and out there I sought You,
> and I—misshapen—chased after
> the beautiful shapes You had made.
>
> You were with me,
> but I was not with You.
> Beautiful things kept me far off from You—
> things which, if not in You, would not be,
> not be at all.
>
> You called and shouted out
> and shattered my deafness.

---

10 Ibid., p. 178.

You flashed, You blazed,
and my blindness fled.
You were fragrant, and I drew in my breath
and panted for You.
I tasted You, and hunger and thirst for more.
You touched me,
and I burned for your peace.[11]

Now a Christian, Augustine planned to lead a monastic life, but not in the ascetic, body-denying way characteristic of many monastic orders of his time. Rather, he sought a quiet place to retreat and study with a group of friends, his son and his mother. In 391, aged thirty-seven, he was ordained as a priest. Augustine went to see a friend in Hippo (in present day Algeria) and visited a church while there. There was already a local bishop ministering there; however, unfortunately he didn't speak the local language well at all. When the congregation spotted Augustine, they seized him to force him to be priest of that church. He cried as they led him up the front of the church; they thought he wept because he was being installed as a lowly priest, not as an honoured bishop, but really his tears were the result of the realization that his dreams of a quiet life were being dashed.

However, despite the reluctant start, Augustine made a wonderful pastor. In 395 he was ordained a bishop of Hippo and he remained there for the rest of his life.

---

11 *Confessions*, 10:27. Harmless, *Augustine in His Own Words*, (2010), pp. 33–4.

As he lay dying at aged seventy-five in 430, Gothic tribes were invading his city. Yet he refused to leave his congregation. He preached to the level of his people on the fringes of the Roman Empire in Hippo, not in an academic way that he was more than capable of. He was deeply involved in the lives of the people of his congregation, and wrote extensively, defending Christian doctrine in the face of opponents, particularly the Manicheans, the Donatists (a breakaway church who insisted they were the 'pure', true Church) and Pelagius. All three denied the nature and power of God's grace in different ways.[12] However, it is to this last, and arguably most important, debate with Pelagius and his followers that we will turn our attention to now, for while the issues of sin and grace are present in all three of the heresies, Pelagianism seems to be the one we are most susceptible to today.

Augustine: the doctor of grace

How Augustine talks about God's grace in the Pelagian controversy has led to him being dubbed 'the doctor of grace.'[13] For someone whom he never actually met in person, Augustine certainly spilled a lot of ink in his disputes with Pelagius. Pelagius was a British monk (some suggest Scottish), who was about Augustine's

---

12 Gerald Bray and Augustine, *Augustine on the Christian life: Transformed by the Power of God* (Wheaton, IL: Crossway, 2015), p. 146.

13 Justo Gonzalez, *The Mestizo Augustine: A Theologian Between Two Cultures* (Downers Grove, IL: InterVarsity Press, 2016), pp. 140-1.

age. Pelagius was described by Jerome, a heavyweight contemporary theologian, as a 'huge, bloated, Alpine dog, weighed down with Scottish oats'—a waistline not quite in keeping with the monastic lifestyle![14]

Pelagius' theological convictions emerged out of a worthy desire to combat the moral laxity of those who ostensibly claimed to be followers of Jesus. He did have a point. Christianity had recently moved from being a persecuted religion in the Roman Empire to more or less being the state-endorsed religion of the Roman Empire. About forty years before Pelagius was born, Constantine, the Roman Emperor at the time, had something of a conversion experience on the eve of a very significant battle in 312. He went on to win that battle, and attributed his victory to Christ. He issued the *Edict of Milan* in 313 which demanded Christianity be tolerated. From then on Christianity gained significant momentum in the Roman Empire, and within a generation the tables had turned for Christians. Whereas previously it had certainly been disadvantageous to be a Christian —the lions of the arena and torches of Emperor Nero's garden parties were fed by Christians —there were now incredible advantages.

All this meant that nominalism wracked the Church. People tended to be culturally Christian, meaning that they were half-hearted in their commitment to Jesus and were living compromised lives. Before, when it could

---

14 Jerome, *Commentary on Jeremiah III*. Quoted in Rees, *Pelagius: Life and Letters* (Suffolk: Boydell Press, 1998), p. 7.

cost you your life to be a Christian, there was little room for being unsure about your commitment to Jesus as your Lord and Saviour. Refusing to denounce Him when asked was tantamount to a death sentence. Little wonder that places in the world where Christians suffer persecution soon weed out people whose commitment to Jesus is ephemeral.

What Pelagius taught

Pelagius saw this lack of holy living amongst churchgoers and wanted to reform the Church. He charged Christians of his day, 'If it pleases you to be a Christian, then perform the works of Christ and adopt the name of Christian deservedly. Or perhaps you do not wish to be a Christian, but just to be called one!'[15] However, his remedy to this issue took him into dangerous waters. Pelagius denied the concept of 'original sin,' instead teaching that human beings are perfectly capable of obeying God fully. Pelagius taught that our wills are free to choose to obey God. Pelagius was particularly inflamed by Augustine asking God to 'give me the grace to do as you command, and command me to do what you will!'[16] That is, Augustine asks God to give him the ability to keep His commands. Pelagius hated this, because he argued that God would not command

---

15 Pelagius, *De vita christiana* 1.1– 1.2. Harmless, *Augustine in His Own Words*, p. 375.

16 *Confessions,* 10:29 (London: Penguin Books, 1961), p. 233.

something that He knew people couldn't keep in and of themselves. In other words, moral 'ought' necessitates moral 'can.'

In 414 Pelagius wrote a letter to a young woman called Demetrias, who had recently become a nun. In it, Pelagius argued that God would not give commandments people couldn't keep:

> [Instead of regarding God's commands as a privilege] … we cry out at God and say, 'This is too hard! This is too difficult! We cannot do it! We are only human, and hindered by the weakness of the flesh!' What blind madness! What blatant presumption! By doing this, we accuse the God of knowledge of a twofold ignorance—ignorance of God's own creation and of God's own commands. It would be as if, forgetting the weakness of humanity—his own creation—God had laid upon us commands which we were unable to bear … God has not willed to command anything impossible, for God is righteous; and will not condemn anyone for what they could not help, for God is holy.[17]

This idea of 'free will' that Augustine and Pelagius battled over came from differing views of 'original sin'. The Church so far had understood that because Adam and Eve sinned, their children and their children's children for every generation would be born sinful. Humankind

---

17 Cited in Alister McGrath, *Historical Theology* (Oxford: Blackwell, 1998) p. 81. See also J. Stevenson, *Creeds, Councils and Controversies: Documents Illustrating the History of the Church, AD 337-461* (London: SPCK, 1989), pp. 233–4.

was *included* in Adam and Eve's sin and needed God's grace to save them and to enable them to obey Him. Instead, Pelagius argued that Adam's sin had no bearing on those who came after him, beyond that of setting a bad example—an example not to follow. Neither the guilt from Adam's sin nor the infection from Adam's sin is passed on down the generations. This meant that Adam and Eve's offspring were perfectly able to make right moral choices. So, Pelagius argued, if people were able to obey God, then they must be able to obey God all the time. Pelagius taught that it was actually possible for a Christian to live a life completely without sinning.

Pelagius did actually have a place for God's grace in his thinking. However, when he spoke of God's grace, Pelagius really had in mind God setting up the right conditions for our right actions. God's grace is evident, for example, in a person's ability to make decisions freely. Pelagius also saw the grace of God as evident in the example of Jesus showing us how to obey God, in the enlightenment received at a person's baptism, and in the gifts of the Holy Spirit. Notice that all these examples of God's grace put the onus on the person to obey God in order to be saved. According to Pelagius, while God's commandments can always be obeyed, it is certainly much easier if God helps us out in these ways. We need to use our natural capabilities that God has given us to obey Him, which means God gets the glory for a person's obedience to Him. Pelagius explained how God alone gets the praise for human obedience: 'Whenever we say that a person can live without sin, we also give praise to God by our acknowledgement of the power which we have received from him, who has bestowed such power on us; and there is here no occasion for praising the human agent, since it is God's matter alone.'[18]

Augustine's response

The Church was quite slow in spotting just how dangerous Pelagius' teaching was. However, Augustine identified the danger and knew he needed to respond. He needed to protect not only the people under his spiritual care in the church at Hippo, but indeed Christians across the Roman Empire. Augustine saw what was at stake—nothing less than the grace of God. He knew that the Bible taught that human beings were indeed sinful from birth and that God's grace was God's unmerited gift to those who trusted in Jesus for forgiveness of their sin. A favourite Bible passage of Augustine's in this controversy was John 15:5, and he used it in refuting Pelagius and his followers, writing that they are 'opponents of the grace of God...that without it, as they believe, man can do all the commandments of God. But if this were true, God would evidently have said in vain, 'apart from me, you can do nothing' (John 15:5).'[19]

---

18 Pelagius, *In Defense of Free Choice*. Cited in Stevenson, *Creeds, Councils and Controversies*, p. 233.

19 Augustine appealed to the Bible to make his arguments, and some of the Bible passages he used in his debate with Pelagius include

Augustine maintained that if a person sinned, it was through *inclusion* in Adam's sin, not because of *imitation* of Adam's sin, as Pelagius taught. While Pelagius did away with original sin, Augustine emphasised that both the guilt *and* contamination of Adam's sin is passed down to us. We come into the world bound up in Adam's sin, and then we go on to fully embrace it ourselves, and therefore commit sin in our own lives. He gave three helpful pictures of what original sin looks like, and how Jesus rescues us from it.[20] First, he saw sin as a power which holds us as prisoners, and from which we cannot break free by ourselves. Therefore, Jesus comes as our liberator to free us. Second, sin is a hereditary disease, passed down in each generation. Jesus heals us as our divine doctor. Augustine regarded original sin as a sickness requiring a physician, writing, 'Human nature was certainly originally created blameless and without any fault; but the human nature by which each one of us is now born of Adam requires a physician, because it is not healthy.'[21] It is only by God's grace that our sickness can be diagnosed as sin, and a cure made available

---

Matthew 20:1-10; Luke 10:30-34; John 15:5; 2 Corinthians 3:6; 1 Corinthians 4:7; and, at the end of his life, he started to pay more attention to Romans 11:5 and was upset at himself for not looking at it more carefully sooner. See Alister McGrath, *Christian Theology: An Introduction* (Malden: Blackwell, 2001), pp. 446–8.

20 For compiling and articulating these three images so helpfully, including the image of the balance pan, I am indebted to McGrath, *Historical Theology*, pp. 80–82.

21 Augustine, *On Nature and Grace*, 3–4. Cited in McGrath, *Christian Theology*, p. 447.

through grace. Third, sin is like being found guilty in a courtroom. Jesus brings pardon and forgiveness from this guilt. To the chicken and the egg argument, 'do we sin because we are sinners, or are we sinners because we sin?', Augustine answers in the strongest possible way, 'we sin because we are sinners.'

While Pelagius was adamant that human beings had a completely free will to obey God, Augustine argued that the human will is thoroughly incapacitated. Augustine was convinced that original sin did not negate our genuine responsibility for our very real choices. Augustine likened a human being's will to a set of balance pans.[22] Back in Augustine's day, before supermarket checkouts could weigh your pears accurately, balance scales were used for trading. Weights were put on one side, and whatever you were weighing was put on the other. When a balance was achieved, then you knew how much your produce weighed. Augustine said that our decision-making ability, our 'free will,' was like this balance pan. One side represented good, the other evil. When the scales (i.e. our wills) worked properly, then weighing up good and evil decisions could be done properly and the right moral decision made. However, Augustine argued that sin had distorted our scales. Like a merchant who loaded all his weights on one side of the scales, our decision-making ability has been loaded with weight on the evil side. Technically, the scales

---

22 See McGrath, *Historical Theology*, p. 80, for this analogy.

still work, but we lean inevitably towards sin. We sin voluntarily, but also out of necessity.

Augustine argued that it is only God's grace that allows the scales to work properly again. God's grace gives them back the free will that Adam and Eve had before the Fall, that is, the ability to freely choose not to sin.[23] Because of God's grace Christians are able to choose to do what is morally right, which they couldn't have done before they were Christians in their own strength. Augustine wrote that 'works proceed from faith, and not faith from works. Therefore it is from Him that we have works of righteousness, from whom comes also faith itself.'[24] Christians will still sin, but Augustine thanked God for the sin he had not committed. He wrote: 'I acknowledge that it was by your grace and mercy that you melted away my sins like ice. I acknowledge, too, that by your grace I was preserved from whatever sins I did not commit, for there was no knowing what I might have done, since I loved evil even if it served no purpose.'[25]

---

23 In regards to the freedom of sinning or not sinning, Augustine argued that in the Garden of Eden Adam and Eve were free to sin, and free not to sin. After Adam and Eve people were free to sin, and weren't free not to sin. In Christ people are free to sin and free not to sin, like Adam and Eve in the Garden. In heaven God's people will be free not to sin, and won't be free to sin.

24 *On Grace and Free Will,* 17. Schaff, *The Nicene and Post-Nicene Fathers. First series. Volume 5: St Augustin: anti-Pelagian writings* (Grand Rapids, MI: William B. Eerdmans, 1971), p. 451.

25 *Confessions,* 2:7. (London: Penguin Books, 1961), p. 51.

Augustine also argued that God's grace is His favour, and as such it is given freely, not because there was anything deserving about the person receiving that grace, but out of God's own free will. He also maintained that God's grace is irresistible—those whom God has chosen to pour His grace out on cannot help but be drawn to it, like a sheep to green pasture.[26] In this sometimes hotly debated area of irresistible grace (a Christian can't help but be drawn to God's grace) and predestination (God chooses us; we don't choose Him), Augustine wrote near the end of his life: 'In trying to solve this question I made strenuous efforts on behalf of the preservation of the free choice of the human will, but the grace of God defeated me.'[27] He landed firmly in the belief that God's grace is freely given; it is totally irresistible, and only God's grace can save a sinner and redirect and remake their will to now want to please God.

Augustine's legacy

Augustine had an enormous impact on the Church right up to today, with B. B. Warfield writing that Augustine 'determined the course of its [the Church's] history in the West up to the present day.'[28] Martin Luther read Augustine's *On The Spirit and the Letter* (based on 2

26 Sermon 131.2. NCP iii/4:137. Referred to in Gonzalez, *The Mestizo Augustine,* p. 145.

27 Retractions, 2.1. Quoted in Chadwick, *Augustine* (Oxford: Oxford University Press, 1986), p. 117.

28 B. B. Warfield, *Calvin and Augustine* (Philadelphia, PA: The Presbyterian and Reformed Publishing Co., 1956), p. 306.

Corinthians 3:6), which was one of Augustine's most important writings against Pelagius. This work greatly encouraged Luther as he challenged the Roman Catholic Church of his day on the issue of grace and justification by faith alone in Christ alone. John Calvin was theologically indebted to Augustine in his *Institutes of Christian Religion*.

In observing Augustine's life we learn that his long journey to Christ testifies to God's relentless grace. He was keenly aware of God's work in his own life before his conversion and helps us reflect on our own experience of coming to know God personally. Augustine also encourages us as we consider people in our own lives who seem so far away from God. Augustine reminds us that it is never too late to come to Jesus, whatever sins we may have committed. Augustine's Christian mother certainly never gave up on her son. Even though from all accounts she was at times overbearing, her consistent, constant prayer for her son's salvation is an encouragement to those who long for someone to come to understand the grace of God for themselves. Augustine is also an encouragement to us that God uses our backgrounds, our skills and our personalities to serve Him in His kingdom.

In observing Augustine's debate with Pelagius we see that it is God's grace that saves us, and God's grace alone. We are utterly incapable of saving ourselves, of pleasing God, of even having the free will to choose to do good, without the grace of God. Augustine reminds us that God's grace means we don't rely on our own strength to save ourselves. Pelagianism is an ever-present danger that we must beware of in our own lives and churches. As a Christian, what gets us into God's kingdom keeps us in God's kingdom. We never move on from the gospel of grace; it is God's grace which saves us, and it is God's grace which keeps us, and God's grace which enables us to obey Him, all through the Holy Spirit's work in our lives. Augustine ends his anti-Pelagian work, *The Spirit and the Letter*, in this way: 'Every mouth should be shut in its own praise, and only opened for the praise of God…For of Him, and through Him, and to Him, are all things: to whom be all glory forever.'[29] Praise God for His grace in our lives!

For further reading

Augustine, *Confessions* (Peabody, MA: Hendrickson Publishers, 2004).

Bray, Gerald, *Augustine on the Christian Life: Transformed By the Power of God* (Wheaton, IL: Crossway, 2015).

For the adventurous

Brown, Peter, *Augustine of Hippo: A Biography* (Berkeley, CA: University of California Press, 1969).

---

29 *The Spirit and the Letter*, 66. Schaff, *Anti-Pelagian writings*, p. 114.

Anselm
Faith Seeking Understanding

IAN J. MADDOCK

Take a stroll around the exterior of Canterbury Cathedral and you eventually come to the southwest porch, famous for its large collection of statues that commemorate important figures in the history of the English Church. Among the Kings, Queens, archbishops and theologians (Jesus is located above the west door, sandwiched between Queens Elizabeth II and Victoria!) stands a statue dedicated to ANSELMVS ARCHIEPISC: Archbishop Anselm. Like many of the fifty-four other carvings, Anselm's likeness hasn't escaped the ravages of time unscathed—though missing only his left hand, he's arguably in much better shape than the headless Thomas Becket!

Anselm stands out among many of his stony compatriots in that he might easily have warranted memorialization as both a churchman *and* a theologian. It's often said that pictures (in this case a 3-D version) can paint a thousand words, and that's certainly the case when it comes to the way Anselm is portrayed at Canterbury. Not only is he dressed in Archbishop's garb, he's also holding arguably his most celebrated theological work, *Cur Deus Homo* (*Why God became Man*). Together, these features go a long way to capturing his multifaceted legacy as one of the most influential church leaders and savvy Christian thinkers of the Middle Ages.

And yet the idea that Anselm should wind up being enshrined so prominently and publicly at the symbolic centre of the English Church is in many ways unlikely. After all, he wasn't even English! Nor (at face value at least) did he aspire to high ecclesiastical office—much the opposite in fact. That being said, as we'll soon discover, Anselm's career trajectory was in other ways 'set in stone' quite early on. He followed a trail—both physical and vocational—that had been blazed for him, one that took him from continental Europe to England and from the quiet scholarly life to negotiating treacherous and complex church-state relations on an international stage. But that's getting ahead of ourselves ...

Anselm, the Benedictine Theologian-Monk

Anselm's story began a long way from Canterbury Cathedral. Born around 1033 in the Alpine town of Aosta in northern Italy, he was drawn to the secluded life of the monastery from an early age. His father, however, a Lombard nobleman named Gundulf, saw his son's future in politics. This became a significant point of contention when Anselm attempted to enter the local Abbey at age fifteen. Being so young, Anselm's acceptance depended on his father's consent—which he refused to give. It seems the resulting fracture in their relationship proved insurmountable. Following his mother's death, in 1056 Anselm left home in search of a new life, spiritual and intellectual stimulation—and possibly even a replacement father figure!

After crossing the Alps and spending three years wandering about France, in 1059 Anselm reached the Benedictine monastery at Bec in Normandy. It was quite common at this time for inquisitive, capable young men of financial means like Anselm to travel in search of an education. From all accounts, he was magnetically drawn by the prospect of being mentored by the local prior—the renowned scholar, Lanfranc (1010–1089)—whose influence had quickly helped establish this relatively new religious institution as a hub of learning and piety. To say that Lanfranc's influence on Anselm's life would prove to be life-changing is an understatement.

Anselm didn't need much convincing to put down roots at Bec and in 1060 he realised his long-standing dream of becoming a monk. He quickly became Lanfranc's protégé, known not only as a precociously talented budding scholar, but also for his personal holiness. While Anselm would go on to become the first great theologian of the Middle Ages and arguably the intellectual father of what became known as Scholasticism (an approach towards theology that placed a heavy emphasis on the use of faith-driven reason), his dense treatises are often infused with rich devotional prayers, a deep union of heart and head. His burgeoning reputation was such that when Lanfranc was offered a 'promotion' and called to serve as abbot at nearby Saint Etienne in Caen in 1063, Anselm stood out as his obvious successor as prior (effectively the monastery's most senior lecturer). If Anselm's meteoric rise didn't exactly endear himself to some of his peers (as a 'recent' arrival he had well and truly jumped the unofficial hierarchical queue), it seems he quickly won over his detractors through a combination of humility and unrivalled ability.

But if Anselm was Lanfranc's natural replacement, that's not to say he aspired to higher office, much less relished its demands. And yet, even though he didn't seek this position of responsibility, there's little doubt responsibility sought him—and not for the last time! In fact, unsuccessfully avoiding institutional leadership would become a defining feature of Anselm's life from this point forward. His reluctance—now and later—emerged from a view of life that privileged the spiritual over the material. As far as he was concerned, the inevitable administrative duties that came with institutional leadership threatened to distract him from the real business of (monastic) life: reading, reflection, prayer and scholarship.

Anselm spent much of his fifteen years as prior of Bec teaching theology and mentoring other monks. Towards the end of his tenure he managed to commit some key aspects of his lectures to writing, producing two of the three major works for which he would become known today. The first, completed around 1076, was called *Monologion*. Originally entitled *An Example of Meditation on the Grounds of Faith*, Anselm's goal was to make a case for the reasonableness of God's existence. In an era that looked disapprovingly on theological creativity and innovation, his method was very similar to the one Augustine had taken centuries earlier. While Anselm's approach may sound strange to our ears, it was founded on the Platonist philosophical assumption, commonly held during the eleventh century, that the 'universal' is more real than any tangible manifestation of that ideal. He argued:

> [A]ll the other good things are good through something other than what they themselves are, while this thing alone is good through itself. But nothing that is good through something other than itself is equal to or greater than that good which is good through itself. The one thing, therefore, that is good through itself is the one thing that is supremely good. For the supreme is that which so overtops the others that it has no equal and no superior. But what is supremely good is also supremely great. There is therefore one thing

that is supremely good and supremely great, and this is of all the things that exist, the supreme.[1]

In other words, there is an ultimate immaterial Good against whom we measure all relative material goodness—and that Good is God Himself.

Anselm finished his second major work, *Proslogion*, shortly afterwards in 1078. It was originally called *Faith Seeking Understanding* (*fides quaerens intellectum*) and its title offers an important glimpse into Anselm's approach towards theology. Far from trying to reason his way to God, Anselm was up front that love for God is the only sure foundation for right thinking about God. He wrote:

> I do not try, Lord, to attain to Your lofty heights, because my understanding is in no way equal to it. But I do desire to understand Your truth a little, that truth that my heart believes and loves. For I do not seek to understand so that I may believe; but I believe so that I may understand. For I believe this also, that 'unless I believe, I shall not understand.'[2]

With this framework in place, Anselm went on to offer what he hoped would definitively prove not only God's existence, but also the irrationality of the fool who says in his or her heart that there is no God (cf. Ps. 14:1). Once

---

1   B. Davies and G.R. Evans (eds.), *Anselm of Canterbury: The Major Works* (Oxford: OUP, 1998), p. 12.

2   Ibid., p. 87.

again, Anselm's arguments are consistent with widely held medieval thought categories, this time those first put forward by the Roman Stoic philosopher Seneca, who had described God as being 'that than which nothing greater can be thought.'

Anselm's so-called 'ontological argument' for God's existence is his attempt to establish a stand-alone defence of the necessity of God's existence. It moves from the 'being' (*ontos*) of God to His actual existence. He begins with the idea of a being that is greater than we can think of—a perfect being. From there he reasoned that to exist in reality is greater than merely to exist in thought. If these first two propositions are true, it therefore stands to (faith-constrained) reason that this perfect being actually exists. In Anselm's own words:

> If then that-than-which-a-greater-cannot-be-thought exists in the mind alone, this same that-than-which-a-greater-*cannot*-be-thought is that-than-which-a-greater-*can*-be-thought. But this is obviously impossible. Therefore, there is absolutely no doubt that something-than-which-a-greater-cannot-be-thought exists both in the mind and in reality. And certainly this being so truly exists that it cannot be even thought not to exist. For something can be thought to exist that cannot be thought not to exist, and this is greater than that which can be thought not to exist. Hence, if that-than-which-a-greater-cannot-be-thought can be thought not to exist, then that-than-which-a-greater-cannot-be-thought is not the same as that-than-which-a-greater-cannot-be-thought, which is absurd. Something-than-which-a-

greater-cannot-be-thought exists so truly then, that it cannot be even thought not to exist. And You, Lord our God, are this being.[3]

Here, in a nutshell, is the essence of Anselm's ontological argument. If God is 'that than which nothing greater can be thought' (that is, perfect), He must also necessarily exist. Why? Because if He didn't exist, He wouldn't be perfect. If there was even a possibility of God's non-existence, then His status as 'that than which nothing greater can be conceived' would be fatally compromised. As a (reasonable) result, only God can be thought of as necessarily existing.

If Anselm hoped this would settle the question of God's existence once and for all, he was sadly mistaken! Critics of his ontological argument have been queuing up to deconstruct this 'proof' ever since it first appeared. For instance, fellow-monk Gaulino argued that just because a person has the idea of a perfect island doesn't mean that island necessarily exists in reality. A person can imagine that they have $100 in their pocket, but that doesn't necessarily mean that they do, argued Immanuel Kant in the nineteenth century. The illustrations are different, but the critique is the same. There is potentially a huge gulf between idea and reality; they don't necessarily coincide.

---

3   Ibid., pp. 87-8.

But as Anselm was preparing to respond at length to Gaulino's critiques (the thrust of his defence was that God's intrinsic existence is of a different quality to the existence of created things: God *necessarily* exists, perfect islands don't), this period of intense scholarly output ground to a halt when Herluin, Bec's knight-turned-founding-abbot, died in 1078. Anselm was next in line to fill the leadership vacuum. His natural instinct was to step back, but instead he was strongly urged to step up. 'Avoid office if you can' was Anselm's preferred course of action, but it was once again proving to be a motto too aspirational for him to reach! And so, the reluctant prior became an even more reluctant abbot as administrative duties threatened to take up most of the discretionary time he may otherwise have devoted to mentoring and writing.

His new role didn't only take up precious time; it also took Anselm to England. After William the Conqueror successfully invaded England in 1066, he began to install Normans in positions of importance throughout the country. As a newly minted abbot of a Norman monastery, Anselm was now no longer simply a humble monk; all of a sudden he was now a feudal lord! In the same year he was appointed abbot, Anselm crossed the English Channel, touring land that had been given to Bec and receiving oaths of fealty. While abroad, he also took the opportunity to resume his relationship with his mentor, Lanfranc. A decade earlier, as part of his program of Norman colonization, William had invited Lanfranc to leave France and take up the position of Archbishop of Canterbury. It would prove to be a portentous appointment for Anselm, paving the way for his own subsequent career moves.

Anselm, the reluctant Archbishop

Everywhere he went it seems Anselm made a big impression, and England was no exception. When Lanfranc died in 1089, the English clergy saw in the Archbishop's successor at Bec his obvious successor at Canterbury. A stalemate ensued for the next four years during which Anselm stalled and William II (also known as William Rufus) enjoyed the revenue of the vacant archbishopric for far longer than the customary twelve months. Things came to a head in March 1093 when the king became gravely ill. Fearing that unless he immediately filled the position he would be in danger of hell, he made the crowd (and clergy)-pleasing choice and elected Anselm who was conveniently already in England, once again dealing with Bec-related business.

During the Middle Ages it was considered normal for candidates for high office—especially ecclesiastical high office—to make a show of protest as evidence of their unworthiness for the role. Anselm took his objections to the extreme! The king was bed-ridden and immobile in Gloucester and, since time was of the essence, Anselm was hand-delivered to him. Just as Gregory the Great had reportedly been seized and dragged to the throne of St Peter in 590, Anselm describes having to be carried against his will to his encounter with Rufus, even refusing to grasp the episcopal staff that was pressed against his closed fist.

It wasn't until later in the year that Anselm was officially enthroned and consecrated as Archbishop at Canterbury, but not before he had received the unenthusiastic consent of his monks back in Normandy and negotiated the terms of his installation with the now-recovered king. No doubt grieved by the secular arm-twisting involved in his own installation, Anselm's main demands centred on reordering church-state relations. The reforms he hoped to make were aimed at preventing rulers like William Rufus from intruding upon the spiritual jurisdiction of the Church (for example, when it came to decisions like the appointment of bishops). But while the king initially agreed to restore lands that he had seized from Canterbury, acknowledge Anselm as his supreme spiritual authority in England and pledge allegiance to Urban II as Pope, both he and his successor Henry I were far less amenable in practice.

Given that Anselm didn't hide where his prime allegiance lay (the Pope always trumped the king), his relationships with these kings was bound to be fractious—so fractious in fact that Anselm spent multiple periods in exile. He was no political animal, and the job description of Archbishop required having a stomach for political manoeuvrings that instead often left Anselm feeling physically ill. On one occasion, Anselm refused to give William Rufus a large sum of money to pursue a military campaign in Normandy on the grounds that it would place undue burden on his tenants. In turn, when Anselm made three requests to visit Rome so he could receive his pallium (part of an Archbishop's official dress), Rufus denied him permission every time on the ostensible grounds that he didn't recognise Urban II as Pope. It proved to be three strikes and you're out. In 1097 Anselm decided to leave anyway, whether Rufus liked it or not. He did so knowing full well that, as long as the king lived, it likely meant he would be unwelcome back in England.

Anselm on the atonement

If anyone else might have been dejected by this turn of events, not Anselm! He welcomed exile with relief. For one thing, it enabled him to travel back to his native Italy. He also hoped it would strengthen his self-made case for being relieved of his position as Archbishop. But not only did Urban refuse his desperate plea, he co-opted Anselm's prowess as a theologian and sent him to the Council of Bari to defend the so-called *filioque* clause: the Western Church's position that the Holy Spirit eternally proceeds from both the Father *and* the Son. In addition to spending time in Rome as Urban's celebrity theologian-guest, in the summer of 1098 Anselm enjoyed a two-month writing retreat in the small mountain village of Liberi where he was able to complete a legacy-defining project he'd been working on intermittently since 1092, entitled *Cur Deus Homo* (or, *Why God became Man*).

Over the course of an extended 'dialogue' between Anselm and one of his monks named Boso (Anselm's friend turns out to be far more theologically astute than his name suggests!), Anselm makes a case for the necessity of Jesus' incarnation and its link with the atonement in a way that was nothing short of ground-breaking for his time and place in the history of the Church. The prevailing view at the time—one held as far back as Gregory of Nyssa during the fourth century—was known as the 'ransom theory.' This held that by fallen nature we're held captive by the devil. God offers Jesus as the ransom price for our release. Lured by the 'bait' of Jesus' miracle-working power, Satan tries to consume Jesus but winds up getting more than he bargained for, swallowing not only Jesus' humanity, but unwittingly, His deity too. In Gregory's theory, God tricks Satan into biting off more than he could chew, and in the process, his own self-destruction: Jesus' subsequent resurrection not only secures our freedom but also breaks the power of Satan's chains forever.

Anselm's 'satisfaction' theory offered something completely new: it wasn't Satan who was owed something, but God. As Anselm read the Bible, he recognised that humanity's core problem is sin. He described sin as our failure to give proper honour to God. It was a way that must have instantly resonated with his medieval feudal context where restitution of honour was the prevailing way of viewing relationships. 'To sin is nothing other than not to give God what is owed to him... someone who does not render to God this honour due to him is taking away from God what is his, and dishonouring God, and this is what it is to sin,' wrote Anselm.[4]

This in turn raises the conundrum that lies at the centre of the atonement: how can God be merciful in forgiving our sins and at the same time remain just? Anselm asks:

> But how do you spare the wicked if You are all-just and supremely just? For how does the all-just and supremely just One do something that is unjust? Or what kind of justice is it to give everlasting life to him who merits eternal death? How then, O good God, good to the wicked, how do You save the wicked if this is not just and You do not do anything which is not just?[5]

A number of potential 'solutions' are offered and then rebutted. Why can't God just forgive and forget when we repent, asks Boso? 'You have not yet considered how heavy the weight of sin is,' Anselm famously responds.[6] Or couldn't we just pay the debt ourselves, asks Boso? That's impossible, replies Anselm: we owe God more than we could ever possibly repay. And besides, it's not simply our lack of ability to pay back the honour we've

---

4   Ibid., p. 283.

5   Ibid., p. 91.

6   Ibid., p. 305.

stolen from God that holds us back; our sin makes us fundamentally *unwilling* to honour God as well.

Where then does the solution to the atonement equation lie? In short, the only hope fallen humanity has of being saved is through the death of a God-Man. If no one can pay the debt we owe except God, and no one ought to pay except man, then, reasons Anselm, 'a God-Man should bring about what is necessary.'[7] QED! With Boso acting as a proxy for the once-sceptical reader now fully persuaded by the unrelenting atonement-driven logic for the incarnation ('The road, fortified on both sides by logic, along which you are leading me is such that I see I cannot depart from it either to the right or to the left'),[8] Anselm's conversation partner summarises:

> The substance of the question was: why God became man, so that he might save mankind through his death, when it appears that he could have done this another way. You [Anselm] have responded to this question with so many cogent lines of reasoning, and have thereby shown that it was not right that the restoration of human nature should be left undone, and that it could not have been brought about unless man repaid what he owed to God. This debt was so large that, although no one but man owed it, only God was capable of repaying it, assuming that there should be a man identical with God. Hence it was a necessity that God should take man into the unity of his person.[9]

7   Ibid., p. 321.

8   Ibid., p. 325.

9   Ibid., p. 348.

The 'satisfaction' theory was nothing short of an atonement-theory gamechanger. It single-handedly shifted the conversation from a supposed transaction between God and the devil to something occurring between humanity and God. Some critics have pointed to the way Anselm's attempt to contextualise his theology for a feudal audience meant his focus wound up being on the satisfaction of God's honour rather than on the more biblical category of God's justice. And yet for any of the satisfaction theory's shortcomings, there's little doubt *Cur Deus Homo* was instrumental in paving the way for the Reformers in their efforts to recover penal substitution from Scripture four centuries later.

Anselm was still enjoying his invigorating exile when news arrived that first Urban II, and then William II, had both died. Rufus' death was particularly memorable, shot by an arrow on a hunting expedition in August 1100 (was it an accident? an assassination?). In any event, his younger brother, Henry I, didn't waste any time seizing the throne for himself. Lured by the new king's promise to be more deferential towards the authority of the Church and its new Pope, Paschal II, Anselm returned 'home' only for history to repeat itself. Once again he found himself caught in a tug-of-war between competing allegiances. While he was prepared to grant the king authority to invest bishops with land and property, Anselm pushed back against the king investing bishops with their spiritual authority: that was the Pope's jurisdiction. And so once again, Anselm found himself in exile, before Paschal II and Henry I eventually came to an uneasy settlement that allowed him to safely re-enter England in 1106.

By now Anselm was into his eighth decade and the stress of his role as Archbishop was taking a heavy toll on his body: it seems threatening Henry I with excommunication was not conducive to his physical and emotional well-being! As was his habit, Anselm found refuge in the disciplines of the monastery. While the thought of intense theological reflection might have been burdensome for some, Anselm still found it rejuvenating. In 1108 he even managed to complete an exploration of the thorny relationship between God's sovereignty and our freedom entitled *De Concordia*. Although Anselm desperately wanted to live long enough to complete yet another treatise (this one focusing on the origin of the human soul), in the end his failing health wouldn't allow it. While his mind was still strong, his body was weak. Anselm's first biographer and fellow-monk, Eadmer, who for much of the previous fifteen years had been his almost constant travelling companion, describes how Anselm died 'as dawn was breaking on the Wednesday before the institution of the Lord's Supper, on April 21 in the year of our Lord's Incarnation 1109, which was the sixteenth year of his pontificate, and the seventy-sixth of his life.'[10] He was initially buried at Canterbury Cathedral (adjacent to Lanfranc, appropriately), but

---

10 Ibid., p. x.

the precise whereabouts of Anselm's remains today are unknown.

Anselm's legacy

Anselm's life ended up a long way from the rural Italian town of his youth. He also ended up as one of the most celebrated theologian-churchmen of his age. Like all of us in some measure, he was a product of his religious and cultural environment, and yet his legacy has transcended the medieval European context in which contributions were forged.

His life embodied a whole host of contrasts. Although he didn't aspire to public life, he wound up being one of the most influential Christians of the Middle Ages. In an era that didn't encourage creative thinking, he single-handedly advanced a theological revolution in the way the Church understood the nature of the atonement. As a monk, he privileged the spiritual world over and against the physical, and yet he spent much of his life navigating very material (and high-stakes!) relationships between secular and religious authorities at the highest levels. He was profoundly aware that true knowledge of God is impossible apart from faith, and yet was a champion for the reasonableness of cherished Christian convictions, including God's goodness and existence, and the incarnation of Jesus. Although Anselm's world was very different from our own, his commitment to 'faith seeking understanding'—a deeper knowledge of God motivated by a humble dependence on God—is one that we can aspire to just as much as he did.

For further reading

G.R. Evans, *Anselm* (London: Geoffrey Chapman, 1989).

For the adventurous

R. Southern, *Saint Anselm: A Portrait in a Landscape* (Cambridge: CUP, 1990).

Martin Luther
Here I Stand!

STUART COULTON

A visit to Rome

In the winter of 1510, only a stone's throw from the great Basilica of St John Lateran, Rome, a devout young German monk called Martin Luther joined other pilgrims in falling on his knees and climbing to the top of Pilate's Steps. It was believed that these were the steps on which Jesus had stood when he appeared before the Roman governor Pontius Pilate. They had been brought to Rome in the fourth century by Helena, the mother of the first Christian Roman Emperor, Constantine. For centuries the steps had been regarded as a holy relic, and climbing them as an act of great religious merit. Even today, crossing a busy thoroughfare from the Church of St John Lateran visitors can still climb the steps on their knees—some with an obvious heartfelt devotion and others with a focus on the video camera recording their ascent for posterity!

In Luther's day it was believed that climbing Pilate's Steps could help deliver a soul from purgatory. Luther recited the Lord's Prayer and kissed each step as he made his way slowly up the staircase. His anguished cry when he reached the top—'who knows if it is really true'[1]—gives insight into the spiritual struggle that was raging in his heart and mind.

The visit to Rome was disillusioning for Luther. His experience as a pilgrim to the Eternal City left him with a sour taste. In fact he later said that he went to Rome with onions and returned to Germany with garlic. For Luther that was a bad bargain!

Luther came to Rome with great anticipation for the religious blessing he expected it to be. A visit to such a holy place meant the opportunity to perform acts of piety, which could be applied to family members suffering in the torments of purgatory. Luther recalled that he regretted that his parents were still living when he travelled to Rome. Had they been dead his good works could have freed them from their purgatorial punishments! Even allowing for some typical Luther exaggeration, his point is clear. Luther's expectations were high for what religious benefit could be gained from a visit to Rome.

He visited as many of the major churches as he could, celebrating Mass and saying prayers. He visited

---

1   Heiko A. Oberman, *Luther: Man between God and the Devil*, trans. Eileen Walliser-Schwarzbart (New Haven, CT: Yale University Press, 1989), p. 147. These were the words Luther's son, Paul, remembered his father using to describe (in 1544) his reaction on reaching the top of the stairs.

the Basilica of St John Lateran, but the church was so crowded with pilgrims and priests celebrating Masses that Luther couldn't even get into the church. With typical dry wit he wrote that instead he ate smoked herring![2]

Luther was shocked at the frivolous disregard for the things of God and the blatant evil which he saw around him. So-called religious people in Rome simply laughed at sin and mocked anyone who took offence at irreligion. For the troubled, earnest monk that was as bad as it could get.[3] Monks were paid to celebrate Masses (often for the dead) and so rushed through the service with a speed that shocked Luther. Whilst he was completing one Mass some were finishing their sixth or seventh![4] He likened them to jugglers in the speed with which they tossed off one Mass after another. Sometimes they yelled at him to hurry up. Others mocked the Mass, reciting in Latin not the words of consecration but rather:

Bread you are, bread you shall remain; wine you are, wine you shall remain.[5]

---

2   Martin Luther, 'Preface to Commentary on Psalm 117,' in *Luther's Works*, American Edition (55 vols.; ed. Jaroslav Pelikan and Helmut T. Lehmann; Philadelphia, PA: Muehlenberg and Portress, and St Louis: Concordia, 1955–86), 14:5.

3   Luther, 'On the Papacy in Rome Against the Most Celebrated Romanist in Leipzig,' in *LW*, 39:59.

4   Luther, 'Rival Claims for Tombs of the Apostles, Summer or Fall, 1542,' in *LW*, 54:427.

5   Luther, 'The Private Mass and the Consecration of Priests, 1530,' in *LW*, 38:166.

Luther described himself as a devout young monk who was deeply offended by such attitudes.

Luther's struggle

How did Martin Luther come to be so zealous to fulfill all religious righteousness and so despondent with what he saw and experienced?

Martin Luther was born in Eisleben, around 1483. Whilst his mother, Margarethe, could recall the day (November 10), she was uncertain of the year! His family might be described in today's language as aspirational. Luther's father came from a peasant farming family. However, his future lay in copper mining where Hans Luther was able to establish himself with a small measure of material success. It was sufficient for Hans to dream of his son becoming a lawyer.

In 1501, as a seventeen year old, Luther arrived to study at the University of Erfurt. Having first completed an Arts degree, he then enrolled in law. It was whilst studying law that Luther made the decision to become a monk. Years later, on the thirty-third anniversary of his entering the monastery, Luther looked back on the circumstances that led him to such a decision. Only a few weeks into his legal studies, Luther had returned home to his parents in Mansfield. The reason for his visit so early in the first term is unclear. It may have been to make arrangements for Luther to marry. If so, then the thought of an approaching marriage may well have given sharper focus and greater urgency to Luther's thinking. Returning to Erfurt from his parents' home, on July 2, 1505, Luther was caught in a thunderstorm some six kilometres from his destination. A bolt of lightning struck close enough to cause him to cry out in fear to St Anne, promising to become a monk in exchange for her aid. He admitted to later regretting the vow, but nonetheless he was determined to honour it.[6]

It was a very medieval thing to do. The notion of appealing to patron saints had grown gradually over many centuries. Calling upon St Anne was an obvious choice for Luther to make. She was considered to be the saint for miners (Luther's father was a miner). It is unlikely that the promise to St Anne was a bolt from the blue. In all likelihood Luther had been contemplating this course of action for some time.

Luther's experience as a monk shows a man tormented both by the holiness of God and his own inability to live in such a way that he could have confidence God would accept him. This spiritual struggle in Luther is unlikely to have begun after he had made the decision to enter the monastery. More likely, it was a part of the process by which Luther decided to become a monk.

By the early sixteenth century, monasteries were regarded by many as places of indulgence and excess. Stories abounded of drunkenness and gluttony within monasteries. Luther came to the monastery to save his soul:

---

6   Luther, 'Table Talk, No. 3707,' in Ernest Gordon Rupp & Benjamin Drewery, *Martin Luther* (London: Edward Arnold, 1970), p. 2.

I took the vow not for the sake of my belly but for the sake of my salvation, and I observed all our statutes very strictly.[7]

It was an intensely personal issue, a matter of the soul. Whatever the bargain he was negotiating with St Anne during the thunderstorm, it was salvation that Luther was pursuing when he knocked at the doors of the Augustinian monastery in Erfurt on July 17, 1505.

For Luther, though, the monastery proved to be something of a nightmare. Whilst excelling at his studies (he eventually was awarded a doctorate in his theological studies and lectured students for the bulk of his adult life), Luther struggled with the burning question—How could he ever be right with the holy God, when he fell so far short of God's standards?

For many years as a monk Luther did everything required of him. When he claimed to have kept all the statutes of his Order strictly he was not exaggerating:

... I almost fasted myself to death, for again and again I went for three days without taking a drop of water or a morsel of food. I was very serious about it ... I chose twenty-one saints and prayed to three every day when I celebrated mass; thus I completed the number every week.[8]

---

7   Luther, 'How Luther Stopped Wearing Habit of Monk, March 18, 1539,' in *LW*, 54:338.

8   Luther, 'What Fasting Was Like in the Monastery, March, 20, 1539,' in *LW*, 54:339–40.

As a monk Luther was obligated to pray at set hours of the day (and night). However, he could not always keep up, as the busyness of lecturing and writing took up increasing hours of his day. He would keep track of what prayers he missed and so accumulate a 'debt' of prayers over sometimes two or three weeks. He would then set aside a Saturday or some extended space of time to catch up on his missed prayers. He would later describe it as a 'torment of prayers.'[9] Prayer was a duty that he performed but one that gave him no assurance or peace even after he had done all that was demanded of him. It was a good work that fed his anxiety about whether he was acceptable before God.[10]

Prayer was not alone in feeding Luther's anxiety. A stone relief over the outer door of the former abbey church of St Madeleine in Vezelay, France, shows Christ seated in judgment with His arms outstretched. On His right are those being ushered by angels away to heavenly peace. On His left are those, huddled together and in shackles, who having been weighed in the balance are cast away from Christ, into the hands of Satan. The beauty of the sculpture is in stark contrast with its confronting theme.

Such images were a regular feature of churches in the Middle Ages, providing blunt warnings about the

9   Luther, 'As a Monk Luther Observed Prayers Strictly, Spring 1533,' in *LW*, 54:85.

10 Luther, 'Sermon on the Gospel of St John 15:7,' in *LW*, 24:240.

coming judgment and its grim consequences. Within a largely illiterate society, visual images played on people's religious 'insecurities.'[11] Have I done enough to escape the horrors of hell? How long must I spend suffering torment in purgatory? When my life is weighed in the scales, will I have done enough?

So how did medieval theologians deal with the question: How can I be right with God? Their solution was to apply to theology[12] the philosophical principle that 'only like can know like.' Therefore we can only know God if we are like God. As no one suggested that God would come down to our level, it was clear that we must rise to His—become holy.

The medieval theologians who came up with this idea may have been drawing upon ancient Greek philosophy in their thinking, but it is a biblical concept nonetheless. The Scriptures teach of a God who is holy and judges sin. It is only the holy man or woman who can have fellowship with Him.[13] The critical question, though, is how does that happen? How does a person who is not holy become sufficiently like God to have a relationship with Him that extends beyond judgment into something more life affirming?

The medieval Church's answer was that the sinner needed to engage with the sacraments of the Church,

---

11 Carter Lindberg, *The European Reformations* (Malden, MA: Blackwell Publishing, 1996), p. 60.

12 Lindberg, *European Reformations*, p. 68.

13 Psalm 15:1–2.

like baptism, confession and penance.[14] Penance might be a pilgrimage to visit a holy site or it might take the form of fasting for a set number of days, reciting prayers or even visiting holy relics. The final question was how a person, having gone on a pilgrimage or viewed relics or said prayers and paid for a Mass, might know whether they have done enough to be acceptable before God? After all the confessions and costly penitential activity, how can you know whether you are acceptable to God?

The answer to that question was to *do your best*. Many medieval theologians argued that God promised to accept a person provided they did what 'lay within them.' That is to say that they did their best to be holy.[15] Luther commonly referred (critically) to this maxim as, 'When a man does the best he can, God without fail bestows grace.'[16]

An easy going conscience will be readily satisfied that enough has been done. But if, on the other hand, you have a high view of God's righteousness and an acute awareness of your own weakness—then how can you be sure that you have done everything that lies within you? And how can your best ever be sufficient to satisfy the holy demands of God? Thus

14 Steven Ozment, *The Age of Reform 1250-1550: An Intellectual and Religious History of Late Medieval and Reformation Europe* (New Haven, CT: Yale University Press, 1980), pp. 216-7.

15 Alister E. McGrath, *Reformation Thought: An Introduction*, 3rd ed. (Oxford: Blackwell Publishers, 1999), p. 75.

16 Luther, 'Lectures on Genesis 12:17,' in *LW*, 2:314.

the Church kept people in a state of uncertainty about their salvation.[17]

This answer to sin gave no satisfaction to Martin Luther. As he explained to his congregation in his sermons on John's Gospel:

> I myself was a monk for twenty years. I tortured myself with prayers, fasting, vigils, and freezing; ... [w]hat else did I seek by doing this but God, who was supposed to note my strict observance of the monastic order and my austere life? ... For I did not believe in Christ; I regarded Him only as a severe and terrible Judge, portrayed as seated on a rainbow.[18]

This fear of God's anger was reinforced for Luther every time he went to church. Outside St Mary's Church in Wittenberg, where Luther attended and later preached regularly, was a sandstone sculpture of Christ. It struck terror into the young monk. So much so he was afraid to look at it when he entered the church![19] It is worn down by time today, but it is still possible to see that out of the right side of Christ's mouth is a lily—the symbol of new life and peace, whilst out of the left side of His mouth is a sword—the symbol of judgment.

The image fed into Luther's own insecurity about whether he was acceptable to God, whether he had

---

17 Ozment, *Age of Reform*, p. 216.

18 Luther, 'Sermon on the Gospel of St John 14:1,' in *LW*, 24:24.

19 Lindberg, *European Reformations*, p. 58.

done everything he could. It spoke only of judgment to the anxious monk. No doubt Luther was recalling his own experience of the sandstone figure of Christ outside St Mary's in Wittenberg, when in a sermon on John 2 he said:

> And in the papacy we find paintings which portray Christ with a sword issuing from one side of His mouth and a lily twig from the other; the point of the sword is to be directed against man.[20]

The righteous shall live by faith!

There is much debate as to when precisely Luther made his pivotal discovery which would transform not only his own life, but would reverberate all around the world. At what point did faith alone in Christ alone become the answer to his deep spiritual longings?

It would be a mistake to imagine that Luther arrived at his understanding of salvation in a 'light bulb' moment. Whilst lecturing in Wittenberg Luther had opportunity to engage at depth with the Scriptures—firstly Psalms and then Romans. It was through that study, sometime during the years leading up to October 31, 1517, that Luther's understanding was transformed.

Looking back upon this discovery over these years Luther put it this way:

---

20 Luther, 'Sermon on the Gospel of St John 2:15,' in *LW*, 22:222. For a fuller discussion of this topic see Stuart Coulton *Hitting the holy road* (Nottingham: IVP, 2011), ch. 15.

The words 'righteous' and 'righteousness of God' struck my conscience like lightning. When I heard them I was exceedingly terrified. If God is righteous [I thought], he must punish. But when by God's grace I pondered, in the tower and heated room of this building, over the words, 'He who through faith is righteous shall live' [Rom. 1:17] and 'the righteousness of God' [Rom. 3:21], I soon came to the conclusion that if we, as righteous men, ought to live from faith and if the righteousness of God contribute to the salvation of all who believe, then salvation won't be our merit but God's mercy. My spirit was thereby cheered. For it's by the righteousness of God that we're justified and saved through Christ. These words [which had before terrified me] now became more pleasing to me. The Holy Spirit unveiled the Scriptures for me in this tower.[21]

For Luther the uncertainties of the medieval Church's teaching on salvation were removed. The question of whether he had done enough to be justified before God was answered—No! He could never do enough. God through Christ does it all! Luther recognised that if he was to be declared righteous, then it must be by the grace of God alone, without need, or even the possibility, that he should 'do his best' or contribute to this work.

Luther couldn't keep this breakthrough to himself. It was not only *his* soul that was at stake. Luther's discovery was also for him a pastoral imperative. In his lectures on

---

21 Luther, 'Description of Luther's "Tower Experience," Between June 9 and July 21, 1532,' in *LW*, 54:193–4.

Romans he strongly condemns the sale of indulgences as an act of cruelty inflicted upon ordinary people:

> And the pope and the priests who are so generous in granting indulgences for the temporal support of churches are cruel above all cruelty, if they are not even more generous or at least equally so in their concern for God and the salvation of souls, since they have received all they have as a free gift and ought to give it freely too. But 'they are corrupt, they do abominable deeds' (Ps. 14:1), seduced themselves and seducing the people of Christ away from the true worship of God.[22]

On October 31, 1517 he opened his views up for public debate by nailing a set of ninety-five theses to the door of the Castle Church in the city where Luther taught—Wittenberg. That simple act brought a storm of controversy down around Luther's head!

The focus of Luther's Ninety-five Theses was the Church's traffic in indulgences. The medieval Church identified two forms of punishment—eternal and temporal. Whilst the sacrament of penance was meant to remove eternal punishment, there still remained a temporal punishment, which needed to be paid. In the event that this additional punishment was not *paid off* during a person's lifetime, it would have to be dealt with in purgatory. Since the time of the Crusades, there had been the opportunity for people to earn a reduction in

---

22 Luther, 'Lectures on Romans' in *LW*, 25:409.

the time that they would be required to spend in purgatory through the Church granting them an indulgence—effectively a reduction in temporal punishment. At first it involved the person performing some special good work or religious act—going on a crusade, for example. But gradually it took on a more commercial character and the Church began to sell indulgences. By Luther's day it was big business!

It is not hard to see how Luther's new understanding of the old biblical truth that we are set right before God solely by the work of Christ received by faith would come into conflict with the practice of selling indulgences. In 1517 indulgences were being sold not far from Wittenberg, in a particularly aggressive marketing program that blurred whatever theological distinctions the serious theologians might have wanted to maintain, and appeared to be offering eternal life for sale.

Luther's Ninety-five Theses attacked this abuse. The immediate response from the man behind this aggressive campaign (Albrecht, Archbishop of Mainz) was to complain to the Pope about Luther. Luther was invited to participate in a debate in Heidelberg in April of the following year; was summonsed to be interrogated by Cardinal Cajetan in Augsburg later in 1518; then debated a leading Catholic theologian Johannes Eck in Leipzig in 1519. This flurry of debates led inevitably to a Papal decree being issued against the monk in June 1520 calling upon Luther to recant his teaching or face excommunication. In typical Luther fashion, he publicly burnt the decree!

Luther's formal excommunication occurred in January 1521, followed by a summons to appear before the Holy Roman Emperor (in whose Empire Luther lived). Luther arrived at the Imperial Diet of Worms in April 1521, famously refusing to recant from his teachings:

> … my conscience is captive to the Word of God. I cannot and I will not retract anything, since it is neither safe nor right to go against conscience. I cannot do otherwise, here I stand, may God help me, Amen.[23]

Luther was subsequently placed under an Imperial ban. He was to be considered under the law to be a dead man—he lost all rights and privileges and could be robbed, beaten and even murdered without any legal consequence flowing to the perpetrator. Luther was an outlaw.

At this point Luther's story takes the character of a 'Boy's Own Adventure.' Travelling back to Wittenberg, with the Emperor's ban imminent, Luther was abducted by armed 'bandits.' They were sent by the Prince of Saxony, the Elector Frederick. Wittenberg was within the territories of the state of Saxony (a part of the larger Holy Roman Empire) and Frederick had decided to protect his now famous monk.

For the next eleven months Luther lived in hiding (and much travail) at the Wartburg Castle, until it was

---

23 Luther, 'The Speech of Dr. Martin Luther before the Emperor Charles and Princes at Worms on the Fifth Day after Misericordias Domini [April 18] In the Name of Jesus' in *LW*, 32:112–3.

necessary for him to return to Wittenberg in 1522 to assume public leadership of the revolution he had started. In the coming decades he would draw out the theological implications of his teaching, liaise with church leaders and heads of state, oversee the establishment of a national Church and provide counsel to the countless people who sought his wisdom.

Luther's legacy

Luther has both attracted and repelled people from the earliest days of the Reformation right down to our present day. He was a man of extremes whose deep grasp of God's mercy and strong pastoral concern for others jar against his inflammatory writings about revolutionary peasants and Jews. And the vulgar and the holy were inextricably linked in Luther. He had an acute awareness of the reality of temptation and a robust confidence in God to enable him to face the challenges of the devil:

> I was often pestered [by the devil] when I was imprisoned in my Patmos, [Wartburg Castle] high up in the fortress in the kingdom of the birds. I resisted him in faith and confronted him with this verse: God, who created man, is mine, and all things are under his feet. If you have any power over him, try it![24]

Yet he could be very earthy, even vulgar at other times:

---

24 Luther, 'How to Deal with Specters and Poltergeists, April 1538' in *LW*, 54:280.

When he [the devil] tempts me with silly sins I say 'Devil, yesterday I broke wind too. Have you written it down on your list?'[25]

Most writers devote at best only a few lines to Luther's personal struggles in the Wartburg Castle: Luther hurling an inkwell at the devil; a poltergeist keeping him awake all night by throwing walnuts at the ceiling.[26] Such stories provide some local colour, a metaphor for his struggle, but aren't always treated with the respect they deserve. However strange Luther's struggles with the devil may sound to our twenty-first-century ears, we can only truly understand Luther if we understand that Satan was as real to him as God.[27]

Luther wrote that there are three rules for a theologian: prayer, meditation and temptation/suffering.[28] By the latter he meant the living out of trust in the faithfulness of God to His promises, in the midst of trial and temptation and suffering—*Anfechtung*. Thus:

... [w]hat labor it costs to fight with the devil and overcome him ... I know it well, for I have eaten a bit

---

25 Luther, 'Treatment of Melancholy, Despair, etc., November 30, 1531,' in *LW*, 54:16.

26 Richard Marius, *Martin Luther: The Christian Between God and Death* (Cambridge, MA: Belknap Press of Harvard University Press, 1999), p. 299.

27 Oberman, *Luther*, xvii.

28 Luther, 'Preface to the Wittenberg Edition of Luther's German Writings,' in *LW*, 34:285. Luther refers to these three as *oratio, meditatio* and *tentatio,* or *anfechtung*.

of salt or two with him. I know him well, and he knows me well, too.[29]

Theology for Luther was never merely an exercise of the mind, an academic endeavour. Theology needed to be lived as well as thought. This new understanding for Luther was a turmoil he had lived through, not simply a puzzle he had solved. When Luther spoke of the necessary requirements for theology, he insisted that the Word of God must be central to all theology; that Word must be faithfully prayed upon; it must be carefully meditated upon and it must be lived in the context of suffering, particularly at the hands of the devil.[30] Luther expected that the Word of God, once taken seriously and experienced or lived, would stir up the hostility of the devil. It is Satan's hostility which makes a true theologian.

Luther's discovery of justification by faith alone in Christ alone was not therefore simply the logical outcome of the careful study of the Scriptures. It was a trial. A pitched battle with Satan. A slow and at times agonising struggle to experience and live out the Word of God in the face of the devil's attacks.[31] Finding a date and pointing to it as the moment of Luther's discovery is to

29 Luther, 'The Eighth Sermon, March 16, 1522, Reminiscere Sunday,' in *LW*, 51:99.

30 Luther, 'Preface to the Wittenberg Edition of Luther's German Writings,' in *LW*, 34:287.

31 Oberman, *Luther,* p. 158.

misunderstand the very nature of that breakthrough. This was not a new way of arguing or presenting theology—a new idea. It was *lived theology*, what Luther called *tentatio* or *Anfechtung*—an understanding born out of trial, temptation and even affliction. That is the context for theology and Luther's understanding of justification arose out of his own struggle, his affliction with guilt over his sin as he wrestled with the Word of God and tried to make sense of its meaning.

It was in 1518 at the Heidelberg Debate that Luther first unpacked the implications of his *Anfechtungen* as a way of doing theology. It was a complete paradigm shift from the medieval Church's thinking on theology and ecclesiology. The medieval method was to understand God in worldly terms, as an Emperor or King, drawing direct parallels from our experience of authority in this world, and applying them to the way God works.[32] Men and women, with a little help from God and a lot of hard work, were capable of good works of piety and charity. It was what Luther at Heidelberg called a *Theology of Glory*—a *glorious* God of power and a *glorious* humanity capable of good works that please God.

By contrast Luther's *Theology of the Cross* said that God determines He will be found precisely in the least

---

32 Robert Kolb, 'Luther on the Theology of the Cross,' in Timothy J Wengert, ed. *The Pastoral Luther: Essays on Martin Luther's Practical Theology* (Grand Rapids, MI: William B. Eerdmans, Grand Rapids, 2009), p. 37. Kolb provides an excellent analysis of the contrast between the medieval Church's *Theology of Glory* and Luther's *Theology of the Cross.*

likely places, the last places we might think to look—in a stable discovered by pagan astrologers; a carpenter's workshop; a small triangle of villages—Capernaum, Bethsaida and Chorazin;[33] a Roman cross; a borrowed tomb.[34] That is, in suffering and weakness.

So Luther wrote in his Heidelberg Theses:

> He deserves to be called a theologian, however, who comprehends the visible and manifest things of God seen through suffering and the cross.[35]

The Christian must live this theology of the cross for himself or herself. Luther's theology of the cross is a way of life. In Luther's understanding there is no room for Christian triumphalism that manifests in either a longing for the return of Christendom when the Church dominated society or a prosperity gospel that offers a health and wealth package to all who believe, or in dreams of glorious success in whatever endeavour we may embark upon, including Christian service. Be content to meet God in the shadows of the gallows, in the obscurity of the stable and in the confusion of finding yourself paying

33 Eugene H. Peterson, *The Jesus Way: A Conversation on the Ways that Jesus is the Way* (Grand Rapids, MI: William B. Eerdmans, 2007), p. 206.

34 Robert Kolb, 'Luther on the Theology of the Cross,' in *The Pastoral Luther: Essays on Martin Luther's Practical Theology*, ed. Timothy J Wengert (Grand Rapids, MI: William B. Eerdmans, 2009), p. 41.

35 Luther, 'Proofs of the Thesis Debated in the Chapter at Heidelberg, May, 1518,' in *LW*, 31:52.

worship to the baby Jesus alongside a group of Gentile astrologers!

It is difficult to overstate the influence Luther has had upon the Christian Church and indeed upon our world. The movement he sparked brought about a revolution within the Church and violent disruption in Europe. The Church today, with its many denominations loosely identified as Protestant, is the product of Luther's Reformation. The shape of modern Europe is in part the outcome of the political consequences of the Reformation Luther instigated. The way we think about God and salvation, individual dignity, and personal freedom has all been influenced by Martin Luther.

Finally, Luther reminds us that our study of the Bible, and our reflections upon the deep theological issues of our time, must always lead us into a humble dependence upon God, and a confidence in God and His Word borne out of our own experience of God's faithfulness to us in the furnace of life.

For further reading:

Bainton, R, *Here I stand: Martin Luther* (Oxford: Lion, 1978).

For the adventurous:

Oberman, Heiko A., *Luther: Man between God and the Devil.* Translated by Eileen Walliser-Schwarzbart (New Haven, CT: Yale University Press, 1989).

Thomas Cranmer
Lord Jesus, Receive My Spirit[1]

Rachel Ciano

A death in Oxford

On a cold, rainy Saturday morning on March 21 1556, a crowd assembled in Oxford, England to watch Thomas Cranmer die. Cranmer had fallen from great heights; he had been the Archbishop of Canterbury (a.k.a. number one churchman in the realm), a prolific writer of Protestant thought and practice, a key architect of the English Reformation, and a close confidante of former monarchs King Henry VIII and King Edward VI. Now, however, the tide had turned against him. Catholic Queen Mary was on the throne, and she was determined to purge England of the sin of Protestantism. Cranmer's execution

---

1   Direct quotes in this chapter have some language updated for clarity.

was to be one of her most illustrious moments—the most influential English Protestant of the day reduced to ash.

Cranmer had been imprisoned for two and a half years prior to his execution. During this time he faced immense pressure, and possibly even torture. In October 1555 he was forced to watch two fellow English Protestant reformers—Bishops Nicholas Ridley and Hugh Latimer—burnt at the stake as heretics. On the night before their execution, knowing that both the stake and eternal life awaited, Latimer remarked, 'Though my breakfast will be somewhat sharp, my supper will be more pleasant and sweet.'[2] While at the stake, Latimer comforted and encouraged Ridley, saying 'Be of good cheer, Ridley; and play the man. We shall this day, by God's grace, light up such a candle in England, as I trust, will never be put out.'[3]

Cranmer was brought up to a tower in the prison to witness the brutal deaths of these his cellmates, colleagues, and dear friends. He watched on helplessly as Latimer died quickly, and Ridley slowly and extremely painfully. It was an object lesson in what awaited Cranmer if he didn't recant his Protestant theological convictions. It was recorded that the government's main aim that day was to frighten Cranmer out of his stubbornness, and

---

2   John Foxe, *Foxe's Book of Martyrs: A History of the Lives, Sufferings, and Triumphant Deaths of the Early Christian and the Protestant Martyrs* (New York: Holt, Rinehart and Winston, 1954), p. 236. This narrative is largely taken from Foxe's account of Cranmer's death.

3   Ibid., p. 237.

the crowd watched Cranmer's reaction up in the tower as much as they did Ridley and Latimer. Apparently Cranmer was traumatised by what he witnessed that day, ripping off his cap, falling to his knees and crying out.

A few months later, that object lesson had done the trick. Cranmer soon signed a series of recantations, taking back his long-held Protestant beliefs and convictions (more of that later). However, even though repentant heretics were supposed to be pardoned, Queen Mary still wanted him burned at the stake—he was too big a prize for her cause to issue a pardon. John Foxe in his *Book of Martyrs* says that Cranmer's part in helping Mary's father, King Henry, divorce her mother, Catherine of Aragon, always festered in Mary's heart; revenge was a key part of Mary's execution of Cranmer. Just as Ridley and Latimer before him, Cranmer was also to die the death of a heretic and be burned at the stake, emulating the fires of hell that supposedly awaited all heretics.

The story so far

These events seem so far from our world today. What led to Latimer, Ridley, and eventually Cranmer's awful deaths? The backstory to these grisly events revolves around a break-up and attempted reconciliation. It is the story of England breaking away from the Catholic Church in Rome, and Queen Mary trying to get them back together. It is the story of England starting to embrace the same truths that Luther had rediscovered in the Bible a couple of decades before, and Queen Mary's attempts to undo Luther and other Continental Reformers' influence on England.

Even though Luther was relatively new to the scene, these attempts at biblical reform were not new. Reform had been rumbling in England for some time. In fourteenth-century England, about 150 years before Luther nailed his theses to the door in Wittenberg, the Oxford-based professor and priest John Wycliff and his followers, the Lollards, were vying for reform. Wycliff is often called 'the morning star of the Reformation' in England. Of great significance was Wycliff's work in translating the Bible into English. This was a bold move, and one that got him into a fair bit of trouble with the authorities. The Lollards laboriously copied the Scriptures out by hand (the printing press hadn't been invented yet) and then walked the length and breadth of England preaching and handing out Bibles to people. Many were burned at the stake for their efforts, because the laity were not trusted to correctly interpret the Bible, and the Bible in their hands—worse still, in their native tongue—was considered seditious and dangerous.

William Tyndale in the early sixteenth century continued the work of Wycliff, translating and printing the Bible in English. Johannes Gutenberg had introduced the printing press to Europe by 1450, so the Scriptures could now be disseminated in the people's native language on a wide scale. Tyndale believed that 'it was impossible to establish the lay people in any truth, except the scripture were plainly laid before their eyes in their mother tongue.' He wanted the 'boy that drives the plough to know more of the Scripture' than the pope. Like Wycliff before him, Tyndale was eventually executed in 1536 for his efforts, his final words ringing out, 'Lord, open the king of England's eyes.' The king he prayed for was King Henry VIII, the man responsible for England's break-up with Rome.

King Henry VIII is often known as the monarch with six wives, the manner in which each marriage dissolved fitting into a memorable rhyme—divorced, beheaded, died, divorced, beheaded, survived. Henry was a good Catholic. He even earned the title 'Defender of the Faith' from the pope for his anti-Luther writing, *Defence of the Seven Sacraments*. So why did Henry end England's relationship with the Catholic Church?

The problem lay in his first marriage, or so he thought. Catherine of Aragon was a great wife and by all accounts she and Henry were happy together. However, her fatal flaw was not being able to grant Henry a son. Henry believed a daughter as Queen would not give England the security it required at the time; a new dynasty established by his father, Henry VII after the War of the Roses, was, after all, only a generation old.

With no legitimate male heir, Henry felt sure that he was under God's wrath. Henry feared God was angry with him because Catherine had previously been married to his brother, Arthur. Arthur passed away five months after the wedding, and Henry stepped in to marry Catherine in Arthur's place. Pope Julius II needed to grant Henry special permission to do so, because it went against canon (church) law. However, over twenty years of marriage without a surviving son left Henry thinking that the pope should never have granted him permission to marry Catherine in the first place.

Henry therefore appealed to the pope (a different one by this stage—Pope Clement VII) to declare his marriage to Catherine invalid, freeing him up to marry again and have the opportunity to realise a male heir. However, this new pope was in a bit of a conundrum, being more or less imprisoned in Rome by Catherine's nephew, the Holy Roman Emperor, Charles V. There was no way that the pope was going to allow Henry to annul his marriage to his captor's aunt! It all reads like a good soap opera script, and the story only heated up from here.

If Henry could not get what he wanted from the pope, maybe it was time the Church in England said goodbye to popes forever. England was Catholic, but why should that be so, Henry wondered. He put his best men on it to try and figure out a way he could cut ties with Rome, because he needed theological and legal backing to get out of the relationship.

Thomas Cranmer, a Cambridge scholar and cleric, was one of these men. Henry got Cranmer on board with the project of annulling his marriage to Catherine because Cranmer already believed that the Bible said kings should be in charge of the churches in their realm, not popes. The flipside of this was that Cranmer also believed that all people in the realm owed their loyalty and allegiance to their monarch, not to some foreign church ruler like the pope in Rome. Cranmer was to prove one of Henry's most loyal subjects and greatest allies. Cranmer travelled to Continental Europe to do research at the leading universities there to see what could be done about Henry's predicament. While he was on the Continent, Cranmer was further exposed to Reformation ideas.

While touring Europe researching an exit strategy from Rome for Henry and England, the Archbishop of Canterbury died, and Henry wanted Cranmer to return to England and fill the role. Once consecrated as Archbishop of Canterbury, Cranmer was able to grant the annulment to Henry. When Henry secretly married Anne Boleyn in January 1533, Anne was already about two months pregnant. Cranmer said he only found out about the wedding two weeks later. Henry's marriage to Catherine was declared illegitimate on May 23 1533, and a week later on the 1 June, a clearly-pregnant Anne was coronated Queen of England. Now her child would be a legitimate heir. Unfortunately for Henry (and Anne), after all Henry had undergone to marry Anne and produce a son, on 7 September she gave birth to a girl named Elizabeth.

During this time, the English Parliament was passing Acts (laws) effectively cutting off the English Church from Rome. It was like cutting a rope one strand at a time. The final, decisive cut was the *Act of Supremacy* in 1534. It declared Henry, and the kings and queens of England after him, the head of the Church of England. It was a structural revolution that gave birth to the Anglican Church. It had the English monarch as its head, not the pope.

In the end, the quest for a male heir had led England to break with the Catholic Church. While Henry had his personal and political reasons for this breach, there were reform-minded people around him who took the opportunity to try and bring Protestant ideas to fruition in England. Chief amongst these people was Thomas Cranmer.

Cranmer's agenda for reform

Now that Henry VIII had broken from the Catholic Church in Rome, Cranmer was able to move forward with theological reform and practical changes to church services. However, he could only move within the bounds that the monarch set, and so progress for the Reformation was slow during Henry's reign. Protestant reform sometimes went forward, sometimes backwards.[4] A great

---

4   If you are interested in knowing more about this, check out the fairly Protestant *10 Articles* from 1536, and then the regressive *6 Articles* from 1539, which Protestants called 'the bloody whip of six strings' for its harsh laws against Protestant doctrines. These *Articles* can be

step forward came in 1539, when the first authorised English Bible was placed in every parish church. This Bible was approved by King Henry, and Cranmer would go on to write the preface to the second edition of this Bible the following year in 1540. This *Preface* was a compelling reaffirmation of the Reformation principle of *Sola Scriptura.* In it he wrote:

> Here may all manner of persons, men, women, young, old, learned, unlearned, rich, poor, priests, laymen, lords, ladies, officers, tenants, … virgins, wives, widows, lawyers, merchants … and all manner of persons … may in this book learn all things what they ought to believe, what they ought to do, and what they should not do, as well concerning Almighty God, as also concerning themselves and all other.
>
> To the reading of the Scripture none can be enemy…it is convenient and good the Scripture be read of all sorts and kinds of people, and in the vulgar [common] tongue, without further allegations and probations for the same.[5]

While Henry himself may never have really owned the Protestant doctrines that he had somewhat unwittingly allowed to sweep into England, he seems to have known it was the future for England, appointing Cranmer as tutor and godfather to his son, Edward. When Edward

---

found, for example, in Gerald Lewis Bray, *Documents of the English Reformation: 1526-1701* (Cambridge: James Clarke & Co, 1994).

5   Thomas Cranmer, *Preface to the Bible* 8:9, cited in ibid., p. 239.

came to the throne upon the death of his father, things had lined up for Cranmer to really embed Protestant doctrine into the English Church.

King Edward VI was thoroughly Protestant. Not only that, but key advisors, placed around him to help the nine-year old boy govern, were thoroughly Protestant as well. During Edward's brief six-year reign (1547-53), Cranmer was able to set out clearly Protestant beliefs and practices into various written projects. Most significantly, he produced the Prayer Book (a how-to guide for church services), 12 Homilies (set sermons), and the 42 Articles of Religion (the Church of England's doctrine succinctly summarised).

Cranmer is perhaps best known for the Prayer Books he wrote—one in 1549, and an updated one in 1552. The second one helped clear up some of the language that had confused people in the first one. For example, he replaced the word 'altar' with 'table' to make it clear that the Lord's Supper did not imply the bread and wine transformed, or 'transubstantiated', into the physical body and blood of Jesus. In the Prayer Books, Cranmer outlined clearly how clergy could run the church service, what they could say, and what the congregation could respond with. The Prayer Books outlined regular church services, as well as special services like baptisms, marriages, and funerals.

Most importantly, the Prayer Books were in English, the language that the vast majority of people in the realm spoke. Cranmer and other Reformers understood how important it was for church services and the Bible to be *understood* by the people. This was hard when the Church used Latin for both the Bible and for church services, a language understood by very few outside of the occasional clergyman and scholar. The Prayer Book was to work side by side with the Bible to help teach the people biblical truths. To this end, the Prayer Book contained set passages of Scripture to be read out each church service (there was a daily morning and evening church service at that time), so that over the course of a year, people in church would hear the New Testament read three times, the Old Testament once, and the Psalms every month. It was an 'annual cover-to-cover-diet of Scripture.'[6]

Cranmer's other writing projects included the 42 Articles, which were finally signed off by King Edward in 1553, just weeks before the king died. This was a statement of faith in forty-two points, outlining the doctrine of the newly established Anglican Church. These were revised about ten years later during the reign of Elizabeth I into the 39 Articles, which the Church of England still uses today. Cranmer also wrote 12 Homilies (1547), which were written out sermons for clergy to use in order to assist in ensuring Protestant doctrines were being preached. The first five homilies set out Protestant

6   Tim Patrick, 'Thomas Cranmer: The Reformation in Liturgy,' in *Celebrating the Reformation: Its Legacy and Continuing Relevance*, ed. Colin Bale, Edward Loane, and Mark D. Thompson (London: Apollos, 2017), p. 145.

doctrine; most of the rest of the others set out how Christians were to conduct themselves in light of this.

Cranmer was certainly able to accomplish much for the English Reformation during Edward's six-year reign. However, it was all to come unstuck for Cranmer under Queen Mary I. Mary was Henry's daughter, but was not first in line for succession after his death because Henry wanted a king rather than queen to succeed him. However, as King Edward died without any heirs of his own, the throne went to her (after a brief, nine day period where Lady Jane Grey received support from some powerful people to become the next Queen of England instead of Mary).

Mary, a devoted Catholic, was determined to return England to the obedience of the pope. Mary's staunch Catholicism was helped by the fact that her mother, Catherine of Aragon, was Catholic, being the daughter of the Spanish powerhouse couple—King Ferdinand and Queen Isabella. When Henry VIII cast Catherine off as his wife, young Mary was ousted too. This seemed to only further embed Mary's Catholic allegiances. England's break from Rome had been the cause of untold distress for her, and returning England to Rome was of national and personal interest.

Executing Protestants was part of that overall scheme of undoing the Reformation in England. In fact, she was so accomplished at it that her nickname became 'Bloody Mary', for there were around 300 Protestant martyrs during her five year reign—Cranmer being her most notorious casualty.

Cranmer's tumultuous imprisonment

When Mary became Queen in 1553 Cranmer was urged to flee from England, but he responded that he was 'not afraid to own all the changes that were by his means made in religion in the last reign.'[7] Nicholas Ridley, Bishop of London, issued a warning to Cranmer when Mary came to the throne:

> If you, O man of God, do intend to abide in this realm, prepare and arm yourself to die: for...there is no appearance or likelihood of any other thing, except you will deny your Master Christ.[8]

Ridley's warnings were soon realised. Within two months of Mary becoming Queen, Cranmer was arrested and charged with treason and heresy. The charge of treason came about because he had tried to enact the wishes of Kind Edward, that upon his death, Protestant Lady Jane Grey was to be crowned Queen of England. However, as Mary moved into position as queen, Lady Grey was arrested and eventually beheaded, along with her husband. In this tumultuous era, obedience to one monarch could very quickly become treason towards

---

7   J. Strype, ed., *Memorials of Thomas Cranmer* (Oxford: Oxford University Press, 1854), 3:37.

8   Parker Society, *The Works of Nicholas Ridley* (Cambridge: University Press, 1843), p. 62.

another. The charge of heresy against Cranmer centred on his beliefs about the Lord's Supper. Cranmer had rejected the Catholic doctrine of transubstantiation earlier in his life, and now believed that Jesus was only present in the Lord's Supper in a spiritual, not physical sense.

Cranmer held two doctrines very firmly, which could co-exist under King Henry and King Edward but butted up against each other in an irreconcilable way under Queen Mary. First, he believed that the monarch was the head of the Church in their realm, not a foreign power like a pope. Second, as a litmus test of his Protestant convictions, he believed in a thoroughly Protestant doctrine of the Lord's Supper. We might think it odd that something like the manner of how a person takes bread and wine in a church service could have such profound ramifications. However, for the Reformers, what they believed about the Eucharist, or the Lord's Supper, was a touchstone for so many other Protestant doctrines—justification, salvation by grace alone through faith alone in Christ alone, the atoning work of Jesus, the priesthood of all believers, Jesus now being at the right hand of the Father and not in the physical elements of the bread and wine, etc.

It was on these two positions that Cranmer underwent severe attack at his trial in St Mary's Church, Oxford, in September 1555. Cranmer was first asked to make his profession of faith. He made it very clear what he believed about the monarch versus the pope:

By the scripture the king is chief, and no foreign person in his realm above him. There is no subject but to a king. I am a subject, I owe my fidelity to the crown. The pope is contrary to the crown. I cannot obey both ... the bishop of Rome is contrary to God, and injurious to his laws.[9]

Cranmer argued that if someone could prove to him that Christ's body was physically there in the bread and wine at the Lord's Supper, he would change his mind, but said no one so far had offered an adequate argument to convince him otherwise.[10] He went on to say that those who take part in the Lord's Supper have Christ within them, though not physically, and that lay people should be given both the bread and the wine, not just the bread as the pope insisted.[11] Cranmer wrapped up his trial by declaring the terrible conundrum in his conscience: 'Christ bids us to obey the king ... the bishop of Rome bids us to obey him ... if I should obey the pope, I cannot obey Christ.'[12] He was indicted for both treason and heresy, and handed over to be executed.[13]

---

9   Parker Society, *Miscellaneous Writings and Letters of Thomas Cranmer*. (Cambridge: University Press, 1846), p. 213.

10   Ibid.

11   Ibid.

12   Ibid.

13   The charge of treason was later dropped, and Cranmer was more than a little relieved, as he always saw himself as a faithful subject to the monarch.

Under the weight of barely imaginable pressure in prison and witnessing the deaths of Latimer and Ridley, Cranmer began to waver. He signed a series of recantations, renouncing his Protestant faith. He specifically denied the teachings of Martin Luther and John Calvin, confessed that outside the Catholic Church there is no salvation, and acknowledged the pope as the supreme head—Christ's representative to whom all Christians should submit to. He confessed the Catholic position on the Eucharist (transubstantiation), as well as the other six sacraments of the Catholic Church, and the doctrine of purgatory. He professed that he did 'not otherwise believe than the Catholic Church and the Church of Rome holds and teaches. I am sorry that I ever held or thought otherwise.'[14] His whole Protestant faith lay in tatters. He had taken back everything he had once professed to believe. He had signed away his entire faith and life's work. At this point, Cranmer was truly sorry indeed for ever holding to Protestantism. However, Cranmer's repentance was not enough for Queen Mary.

On the morning of his own execution, people packed into St Mary's Church in Oxford to hear Cranmer read out his last, decisive recantation, 'lest any man should doubt of this man's earnest conversion and repentance … that … all men would understand that you are a catholic

14 John Foxe, *Foxe's Book of Martyrs*, p. 246.

indeed.'[15] All was going to plan and he started as he was expected to. He recited the Creed and affirmed the basics of the Catholic faith. However, he soon started to go off script. The officials soon noticed, as they had a copy of the last signed recantation in front of them.

Cranmer started talking about 'the great thing, which so troubles my conscience, more than any thing that ever I did or said in my whole life.'[16] What troubled his conscience was supposed to be his Protestant beliefs! Instead, he renounced 'all such bills and papers which I have written or signed with my hand since my degradation' (i.e. since he was removed as Archbishop).[17] There in front of his accusers, he recanted his recantations; he took back his denouncement of his Protestant beliefs he had signed in prison.

His accusers were furious. Here was their prize catch, Cranmer, turning their great moment of triumph into a public relations disaster. A huge commotion broke out in the church, but Cranmer persevered in speaking. Amidst the uproar, Dr. Cole who had preached the sermon cried out, 'Stop the heretic's mouth, and take him away.'[18] As Cranmer was pulled down from the stage, he persevered in shouting two of his Protestant convictions that had been a feature of so much of his life:

---

15 Foxe, *The Acts and Monuments of John Foxe* (Vol. 8, Edited by J.S. Pratt. London: The Religious Tract Society, n.d.), 8:86.

16 Ibid., 8:88.

17 Ibid.

18 Ibid., 8:89

> As for the pope, I refuse him, as Christ's enemy, and antichrist, with all his false doctrine. And as for the sacrament [the Eucharist]... my book teaches so true a doctrine of the sacrament, that it shall stand at the last day before the judgement of God, where the papistical doctrine contrary to it shall be ashamed to show her face.[19]

Cranmer was led to the stake; some accounts have him actually skipping lightly ahead of his executioners, now that his conscience was finally clear. He was to be burned at the same spot on Broad Street in Oxford as Ridley and Latimer were burned the previous year. When they got there, Cranmer was composed. He knelt down to pray, and then calmly put off his outer garments, shoes and cap to prepare for the flames. He reached out to grasp the hands of some of his supporters, saying goodbye to them.

When Cranmer had spoken at the church, he promised that 'for as much as my hand offended, writing contrary to my heart, therefore my hand shall first be punished; for when I come to the fire, it shall first be burned.'[20] Now at the stake, Cranmer made good on his word. As the flames started to leap up, he put his right hand, the one that had signed the recantations of his Protestant faith, into the flames. He held it there unmoving, except once to wipe his face. It is this moment

---

19 Ibid., 8:88.
20 Ibid.

that he has become most famous for, because it was such a clear statement of his final convictions, a sign that could not be misread or undone. Queen Mary's moment of triumph was instead one of despair as news of what happened soon spread throughout England.

Cranmer's Legacy

Thomas Cranmer has received mixed reviews for his involvement in the English Reformation. Some accuse Cranmer of being an inconsistent man, indecisive and pliable.[21] Often, his recantations, and then the reversal of those recantations, are highlighted, with the conclusion that he was weak-willed and indecisive. One person writes, 'Cranmer has traditionally received a bad press. Portrayed as a 'doubting Thomas', Cranmer is seen as a man who in his final hours could not make up his own mind.'[22] Sometimes Cranmer acted with boldness, courage and conviction, and sometimes he acted out of fear and compromise. Amidst it all, he was stuck between doctrines that he believed with all his heart came from the Bible, like his view on the monarchy being the head of the Church in England, not the pope, and his view on the Lord's Supper. These doctrines lined up fantastically

---

21 Bernard M. G. Reardon, *Religious Thought in the Reformation* (London: Longman, 1981), p. 252.

22 Paul Ayris, 'Review Article: Thomas Cranmer and the English Reformation,' *Reformation and Renaissance review*, no. 2 (1999), p. 94.

in some circumstances and dismally in others, depending on who the king or queen of England was.

All this goes to show that following Jesus can be a messy business at times. Cranmer is a very human figure—as we all are. We can succumb to torment; we can buckle under pressure. Cranmer helps remind us that there is truth in the adage, 'the best of men are men at best.' Cranmer was like us—weak, flawed, able to succumb to pressure when our convictions are tested. Cranmer helps remind us that even a great martyr with a fantastic story of dying faithfully holding on to Jesus doesn't mean that the whole of life was lived well up to that point. However, it matters how it ends. Cranmer finished well.

From Cranmer's story we are also reminded that while followers of Jesus may prove unfaithful at times, Jesus is always faithful to His people. This is especially proved true in great trials, and as we face death. John Foxe records that Cranmer was repeating two things as the flames engulfed his body.[23] The first was 'his unworthy right hand.' He hated the fact that in time of weakness he had signed those recantations, and was constantly repenting of that as he died. Second, he used the words of the first Christian martyr, Stephen, continually uttering, 'Lord Jesus, receive my spirit', which echoed Jesus' cry at the cross. Jesus cares about the death of His people, and Cranmer knew it. He also knew Jesus was faithful to him

---

23 Foxe, *Acts and Monuments*, 8:90.

through life and in death. Certain of this, Cranmer died calling on Jesus to forgive him, to receive him with open arms. As Cranmer clung to Jesus in his final moments on this earth, we too can be sure that Jesus is faithful to His promises and will receive us with open arms as we call on Him ourselves.

For further reading

Williams, Leslie, *Emblem of Faith Untouched: A Short Life of Thomas Cranmer* (Grand Rapids, MI: William B. Eerdmans, 2016).

For the adventurous

Brooks, Peter Newman, *Cranmer in Context: Documents from the English Reformation* (Minneapolis, MN: Fortress Press, 1989).

MacCulloch, Diarmaid, *Thomas Cranmer: A Life* (New Haven, CT: Yale University Press, 1996).

Richard Baxter
Keep These Hearts Above[1]

RACHEL CIANO

Richard Baxter was a man with heaven on his mind. It shaped all he did, all he loved, all he thought about—it was like heaven was stamped on his forehead. It was so much at the forefront of his thinking that it didn't take long for him to jump to the subject, whatever the starting point! While preaching at an old and decrepit church in London in 1660, part of the steeple thunderously crashed down. The congregation, who were already scared to meet there because of the dangerous condition of the building, were absolutely terrified by the deafening noise. They ran out of the church in chaotic fear and complete disarray.

Richard Baxter remained perfectly calm, sat down in the pulpit, and waited until the congregation had settled down. When they came back into the church he

---

1   Direct quotes in this chapter have had their language updated for clarity.

picked up where he left off, but first he wished to make the event a teachable moment, saying, 'We are in the service of God to prepare ourselves, that we may be fearless at the great noise of the dissolving world, when the heavens shall pass away.'[2] He wanted the noise of a church steeple crashing down to serve as a reminder of the reality that heaven was coming! He always found a way to get around to the topic of heaven.

An adversity-filled life

While heaven was on his mind, his life on earth was full of adversity. Or perhaps, because his life was full of adversity, heaven was on his mind. Richard Baxter was well acquainted with hardship. Born in 1615, Baxter was no stranger to the trials and tribulations that can come a person's way. Baxter knew adversity by virtue of the time and place he lived. Seventeenth-century England was no walk in the park. He lived under the reigns of five monarchs who each took England in very different directions, especially religiously. Baxter witnessed up close and personal the very bloody English Civil War (1642-51) as an army chaplain. In 1647 he became seriously ill, and for a long time he fully expected to die. He recovered but lived much of his life as a very ill man, often housebound and in severe pain. He wrote

---

2   This story and quote from Baxter were recounted in the sermon preached at his funeral. See W. Farmer, *The Whole Works of the Rev. W. Bates*, vol. 4, 4 vols. (London: James Black, 1815), p. 329.

that relief from pain came 'perhaps once a month for a few hours.'[3]

Later in his life, he was amongst approximately 2,000 Puritan ministers who were forced out of the Church of England in 1662. As a result Baxter was deprived of his livelihood, spent time in prison, faced trumped-up charges in court, and had nearly all his books and property confiscated and sold to pay fines. To top it off, he also lived through the plague of 1665 and the Great Fire of London in 1666. He lived at a very difficult time, especially for those wanting to remain faithful to Christ.

Yet Richard Baxter, in the midst of trials and tribulations, in the midst of pain in his body, in the midst of hardship in ministry and in his personal life such as the death of his dear wife, was able to energetically minister, preach, spend time with people, and write nearly ten million words on all sorts of pastoral and theological issues. How did he accomplish that? Where did he draw his energy from? It seems, from Baxter's own words, that his illness and brush with death in his early thirties is what gave him a sense of how precious his time was, and that he wanted to spend it wisely:

A life still near to Death, did me possess
With a deep sense of Time's great preciousness.[4]

3   N. H. Keeble, *Richard Baxter: Puritan Man of Letters*, *Oxford English Monographs* (Oxford: Clarendon Press, 1982), p. 11.

4   J. I. Packer, 'Richard Baxter on Heaven, Hope, and Holiness,' in *Evangelical Influences: Profiles of Key Figures and Movements*

Baxter's close encounter with death helped focus the rest of his life. It placed everything he did, thought, wrote and said in the context of eternity and heaven. J.I. Packer comments:

> When, like Baxter from the time of his majority [i.e. as a young man], one lives with one foot in the grave, it imparts an overwhelming clarity both to one's sense of proportion (what matters, and what does not), and also to one's perception of what is and is not consistent with what one professes to believe.[5]

That is, because Baxter was acutely aware of his own mortality and therefore how close heaven was, he was able to discern what was important in life, and strove to live in a way that lined up with that. The end destination shaped his journey—it gave him meaning and direction. This is highlighted throughout Baxter's earthly life, and so let's have a look in more detail at the way he fixed his eyes on heaven throughout it.

Fixing his eyes on heaven in ministry

Baxter was ordained as a deacon in 1638, and in 1641 he went to Kidderminster at the invitation of the church there to be a preaching minister. The church had grown frustrated with the vicar in Kidderminster, George

---

Rooted in the Reformation, ed. J. I. Packer (Peabody, MA: Hendrickson Publishers, 2014), p. 227.

5   J. I. Packer, *A Quest for Godliness: The Puritan Vision of the Christian Life* (Wheaton, IL: Crossway Books, 1990), p. 306.

Dance, who frequented the pubs more than the pulpit. He was often found in local taverns, but only preached once every three months. Baxter was therefore chosen to preach in his place.

However, his time in Kidderminster was cut short; after only a year his ministry was interrupted by the English Civil War. The war was between the armies of parliament and the king, who battled one another over the right to rule England and her territories. The Puritans by and large sided with parliament. As a Puritan, Baxter sided with parliament too; however, he still supported the king as a loyal subject of the realm. Unfortunately, this nuance was lost on most people. Near the beginning of the war, Baxter was called a traitor in the street (Kidderminster was in an area that supported the king). Soon, he found he needed to retreat to a nearby town to remain safe, where quite a few other Puritan pastors were in hiding.

Soon things really began to heat up for him. On one occasion, while preaching at a friend's church, he and the congregation were able to hear the cannons and armies fighting nearby. Then the war came closer again to Baxter—or rather, he got closer to the war. Despite refusing at first, he became chaplain in the parliamentary army, which proved to be a difficult time for him. He was often appalled and dismayed by the behaviour and speech he witnessed amongst the parliamentary army. Life on the battlefield was also hard, and he wrote of the 'weary condition of war, and the unpleasing life of a soldier.'[6] He wrote that for four years he witnessed sieges, battles, and distressing sights. The 'sad and heart-piercing spectacles' he witnessed included watching a dear friend fall down in battle in front of him, as well as countless other wounded and dead people.[7]

To be constantly bombarded with the reality of death and destruction around him only encouraged him further to fix his thoughts on heaven. He wrote that there was 'scarce a week without the sight of noise or blood. Surely there is none of this in Heaven.'[8] These thoughts on heaven were about to come into even sharper focus.

About halfway through the war, in the winter of 1647, Baxter fell ill to the sickness that nearly cost him his life and shaped the rest of it. He was told by doctors that he was going to die of the illness that afflicted him (possibly tuberculosis), and started to write out a sermon for himself, meditating on the everlasting rest he believed he was about to enter. He later published these meditations as *The Saints' Everlasting Rest*. As the title suggests, this work is full of reflections on the everlasting rest that God's people will one day experience.

In *The Saints' Everlasting Rest* Baxter writes, 'the saints' rest is the most happy state of a Christian...it is the perfect, endless enjoyment of God by the perfected

---

6   Keeble, *Richard Baxter,* p. 97.

7   Ibid.

8   Ibid.

saints.'[9] On the benefit of thinking about the rest Christians will enjoy in heaven, he writes:

> What [is] more welcome to men under personal afflictions, tiring duties, disappointments, or sufferings, than rest? It is not our comfort only, but our stability. Our liveliness in all duties, our enduring of tribulation, our honouring of God, the vigor of our love, thankfulness... the very being of our religion and Christianity, depend on the believing, serious thoughts of our rest.[10]

Baxter said this time spent meditating on the saints' rest in heaven 'has more benefited me than all the studies of my life.'[11] When he recovered, he knew what a blessing and benefit it had been to him to fix his thoughts on heaven, and so he continued to do it every day for at least half an hour. He also encouraged other Christians to do the same because it is good for them, good for others around them, and it honours God:

> A heavenly mind is the nearest and truest way to a life of comfort...if we would but try this life with God, and keep these hearts above, what a spring of joy would be within us...he whose conversation is in heaven is the most profitable Christian to all about him ...no man so highly honours God, as he whose conversation is in heaven.[12]

---

9   Richard Baxter and Benjamin Fawcett, *The Saints' Everlasting Rest* (Grand Rapids, MI: Baker Book House, 1978), p. 17.

10 Ibid., pp. 16-17.

11 Ibid., p. 8.

12 Ibid., pp. 280-96.

Baxter said to fix a time every day to think serious thoughts about heaven, or it won't get done. He recommended at least fifteen minutes, but ideally 'set apart one hour or half an hour every day' to really be able to get into the zone of thinking and praying.[13] The goal of the session was to 'fire your hearts by the help of your heads...he is the best Christian who has the readiest passage from the brain to the heart.'[14] In typical Puritan fashion, the head was to inform the heart; the mind was to set afire the affections.

In these sessions Baxter said that first, think about your promised rest as clearly and fully as possible in order to feel the emotions that go with it—love, hope, joy, courage and so on. Second, preach to yourself and apply specifically to your own life what you have thought about. 'Imitate the most powerful preacher you have ever been acquainted with...it is a great part of a Christian's skill and duty, to be a good preacher to himself...Two or three sermons a week from others is a fair proportion; but two or three sermons a day from yourself, is ordinarily too little.'[15] Finally, you should move from speaking to yourself, to speak with God which is the 'highest step that we can advance to in the work.'[16] He turned meditations on God into prayer to God.

---

13 Richard Baxter, *The Practical Works of Richard Baxter: Volume III* (London: Henry G. Bohn, 1854), p. 330.

14 Ibid., p. 306.

15 Baxter, *The Practical Works of Richard Baxter, Volume I*, p. 133.

16 Baxter, *Saint's Everlasting Rest*, pp. 382-3.

Once Baxter was back on his feet he returned to ministry in Kidderminster, where he ministered for the next fifteen years, all the way through Oliver Cromwell's Puritan rule over England, Scotland and Ireland, until the monarchy was once again restored. When Baxter arrived in Kidderminster there were about 3,000 people in the town. He described them for the most part as 'an ignorant, rude and revelling people' who had 'hardly ever had any lovely serious preaching among them.'[17] When he started there, he said that 'there was about one family in a Street that worshiped God and called on his name.' However, by the end of his time there in 1660 he wrote that on a Sunday, 'there was no disorder to be seen in the streets, but you might hear a hundred families singing Psalms and repeating sermons' and that there were some streets where the majority of families professed 'serious godliness.'[18] How did the town of Kidderminster transform from such a godless to a godly place? Under God, Richard Baxter brought his heavenly focus to ministry, and as such has often been described as the model pastor.

Puritans were greatly concerned with what a pastor should be like—what kind of person he ought to be, what his priorities should be, and therefore how he should spend his time. Baxter was in many ways the epitome of a Puritan pastor, and indeed any local pastor—he loved

---

17 Baxter, *Reliquiae Baxterianae, or, Mr. Richard Baxter's narrative of the most memorable passages of his life and times,* ed. Matthew Sylvester (London: Printed for T. Parkhurst, J. Robinson, J. Lawrence, and J. Dutton, 1696), Part 1, p. 20.

18 Ibid., I. pp. 84-5.

God, loved God's Word, and loved God's people. Baxter gave his people his head, heart and his feet. His head and heart grappled with God's Word before telling it to others—in sermons, in teaching people week by week in his own house, in writing treatises, books, and letters to people so they could revisit the truths found within them again and again. His feet carried him to systematically visit people in their houses, to speak God's Word to them on sick beds, on their deathbeds, in tragedy and triumph, wherever people needed the balm of God's Word.

Baxter believed that what was most in a pastor's heart would be what was most in a congregation's ears—for Baxter, that was heaven. As a result of his daily habit of meditating on heaven, he constantly preached on this subject to his congregation. He writes in a sort of autobiographical poem how early thoughts of his own mortality shaped his preaching:

> Still thinking I had little time to live,
> My fervent heart to win men's souls did strive.
> I preached, as never sure to preach again,
> And as a dying man to dying men.
> (*Poetical Fragments*, 40)[19]

Being mindful of the realities of heaven also meant that Baxter always had his eye on the unconverted, urging them to repent. He addressed his book, *A Call to the Unconverted to Turn and Live*, to those in Kidderminster

---

19 J.I. Packer, *A Grief Sanctified: Through Sorrow to Eternal Hope* (Wheaton, IL: Crossway, 2002), p. 189.

yet to respond to the gospel, and set eternity before them: 'the eternal God who made you for a life everlasting... [has set] heaven before you.'[20]

As a pastor, Baxter wanted fellow pastors to be transformed by God's Word too, so that in turn they could preach and shepherd God's people under their care. He wrote a handbook for Christian pastoral ministry, *The Reformed Pastor*, which had its origin as a sermon based on Acts 20:28.[21] By 'reformed' Baxter was not referring to a theological system that bears this name, but rather he meant 'reformed' as in 'spiritually reformed' or 'revived'—pastors with spiritual life and vigour in them. Baxter firmly believed that the spiritual state of ministers affected the congregation; if the minister was striving for holiness, the congregation would by and large follow suit. He wrote, 'If God would reform the ministry [i.e. spiritually revive the ministers], ...the people would certainly be reformed. All churches either rise or fall as the ministry does rise or fall (not in riches or worldly grandeur) but in knowledge, zeal and ability for their work.'[22]

---

20 Richard Baxter, *A Call to the Unconverted to Turn and Live, and Accept of Mercy While Mercy May yet Be Had, as Ever They Would Find Mercy, in the Day of Their Extremity, from the Living God* (London: Religious Tract Society), p. v.

21 In Acts 20:28 Paul farewells elders in the Ephesian church, and implores them to 'Pay careful attention to yourselves and to all the flock, in which the Holy Spirit has made you overseers, to care for the church of God, which he obtained with his own blood' (ESV).

22 Baxter, *The Reformed Pastor*, ed. Hugh Martin (London: SCM Press, 1956), p. 10.

Baxter urged congregation members to imitate the holiness of their pastors, and to remember their duty to them—to love them, not to speak or think unworthy thoughts against them, to learn from them, to obey them as they teach faithfully, and to take part in their teaching ministry that he set out in the *Reformed Pastor*. Baxter is an encouragement in our own day of our responsibilities to those God has set over us in pastoral ministry, to love, serve, imitate and submit to them, to not bring them down, but 'remember that the duty which you find belongs to the ministers also shows the duty which belongs to yourselves.'[23]

Baxter wanted to see fellow pastors obtain heavenly focus in their ministries too. 'If we can but teach Christ to our people, we teach them all. Get them well to heaven and they will have knowledge enough…life is short, and we are dull, and eternal things are necessary, and the souls that depend on our teaching are precious.'[24] He chastised fellow ministers, 'How can you preach of heaven and hell in such a careless, sleepy manner? Do you believe what you say? Are you in earnest or in jest? How can you tell people that sin is such a thing, and that so much misery is upon them and before them, and be no more affected with it?'[25]

---

23 Baxter, *The Reformed Pastor*, p. 23.
24 Ibid., p. 72.
25 Ibid., p. 116.

Fixing his eyes on heaven in persecution and grief

In 1660 the monarchy was restored, and two years later Baxter was forced out of the Church of England with around 2,000 other ministers who couldn't in good conscience abide by the *Act of Uniformity*. These laws prescribed how church must be run, including what pastors said and wore at church, and how people participated in Sunday services, the form of which many pastors deemed unbiblical. Baxter considered this 'Great Ejection' of ministers from the Church the greatest tragedy of his life.[26] Until his death nearly thirty years later, Baxter faced a ban on preaching, harassment from the authorities, a terribly hard trial, gaol on several occasions and the loss of his worldly goods through fines.

Christians across England held very different views about how church should be structured and run, however the *Act of Uniformity* meant that there was only one way that was allowed. This fractious climate meant disunity grew amongst Christians, and Baxter laboured in vain for peace and unity. Thoughts on heaven again comforted him in his discouragement. He meditated on the 'communion of saints' in heaven where Christians would be united in their worship of God—in fact, Baxter often talks about the 'communion of saints' as being one

---

26 Packer, *Evangelical Influences: Profiles of Key Figures and Movements Rooted in the Reformation*, p. 233.

of the greatest components of heaven's joy.[27] He wrote of the day he would see the company of God's people in heaven:

> It comforts me to think of that day, when I shall join with Moses in his song, with David in his psalms of praise, and with all the redeemed in the song of the Lamb forever…will it be nothing but beneficial to our comforts to live eternally with Peter, Paul, Augustine… Luther, Zwingli, Calvin.[28]

He goes on to list many of his predecessors and people of his day, all holding very different theological points of view. He pondered with joyful anticipation the Christian peace and love that he would experience in heaven, in days when Christians were more likely to be found at each other's throats!

Two weeks after the Great Ejection, Richard Baxter gave up bachelorhood and married Margaret Charlton. He was by this time forty-six years old; she was twenty-six. Baxter wrote that they lived in 'constant love and peace and concord, except our differing opinions about trivial occurrences, or our … differing modes of talk.'[29] From what we can tell, Baxter's marriage was a happy one. Richard thought the world of Margaret, and was not ashamed to declare her superiority when it came to navigating tricky pastoral situations.

---

27 Ibid.

28 Baxter, *Practical Works vol. III*, p. 43.

29 J. I. Packer, *A Grief Sanctified*, p. 123.

He wrote, 'Her apprehension of such things was so much quicker and more discerning than mine... her reasons and my experience usually told me that she was in the right and knew more than I. She would at the first hearing understand the matter better than I could do by many and long thoughts.'[30]

She was also a loyal companion. 'When I was carried to the common jail for teaching...I never perceived her trouble at it. She cheerfully went with me into prison [and] ... did much to remove the removable inconveniences.'[31] After nineteen years of marriage Margaret died in 1681. A key part of how Richard grieved was to write down her life and death in a memoir, which he said was 'written under the power of melting grief.'[32] During this period, he also made sure that he relied heavily on 'wise friends, whose counsel I have much followed.'[33] He was certain of the biblical portrayal of heaven being where God's people enjoyed Him and each other in never-ending joy, and he was certain Margaret was amongst them. He fully expected, and even looked forward to, his death very soon after hers, but he was to live another ten years as a widower.[34] Meditations on heaven were a great source of comfort to him on this road of grief.

---

30 Ibid., pp. 106-7.

31 Ibid., p. 92.

32 Ibid., p. 145.

33 Ibid.

34 Ibid., p. 153.

Fixing his eyes on heaven in his death

As Baxter neared the end of his life his thoughts of eternity only intensified. In 1676 he wrote *The Dying Thoughts of Richard Baxter*, where he reflected on the Apostle Paul's longing in Philippians 1:23 (NIV), 'I am torn between the two: I desire to depart and be with Christ, which is better by far.' Baxter wrote to a friend that year, telling him that he was indeed writing his funeral sermon on this passage, before adding, 'we never live like believers indeed till the thoughts of heaven be sweeter to us than all our peace and hopes on earth, and till we truly believe that it is better to depart and be with Christ than to be here.'[35]

Dying Thoughts was eventually printed in 1683, nearly forty years after he began *The Saints' Everlasting Rest*, and it contains similar reflections on the certain hope of glory every Christian has. Together they make wonderful literary bookends to his life. In *Dying Thoughts* Baxter emphasised that in heaven, our human natures will be entirely changed—we will be perfected and find what we were ultimately made for. He wanted people to remember 'these plain truths' that 'the world is vanity, that man must die, that riches cannot then profit, that time is precious, and that we have but little time to prepare for eternity.'[36] *Dying Thoughts* was soon read by others—one being the nobleman and politician William

---

35 Cited in Packer, *Evangelical Influences: Profiles of Key Figures and Movements Rooted in the Reformation*, p. 311.

36 Baxter, *The Dying Thoughts of the Rev. Richard Baxter* (London: The Religious Tract Society, n.d.), p. 108.

Russell, who was executed for treason in 1683 but posthumously exonerated. As Lord Russell approached his execution he wrote Baxter a thank you letter for his *Dying Thoughts*, saying that it had 'made me better acquainted with the other world than I was before' and that it had 'contributed to my support and relief, and to prepare me for what I am to go through.'[37]

As Baxter lay on his own deathbed in 1691, he continued to want to encourage people to remain faithful to the Lord Jesus Christ. He said to those who came to him, 'You came here to learn to die. I am not the only person who must go this way…Be sure you choose God for your portion, heaven for your home, God's glory for your end, God's word for your rule, and then you need never fear but we shall meet again with comfort.'

Baxter's Legacy

Baxter's heavenly mindedness is at the same time a challenge and comfort to us living in this world today. He encourages us to mimic him in this most beneficial habit of viewing life through the lens of the end, of thinking of two worlds simultaneously, of seeing life on earth as preparation for heaven. It is Christians who are most heavenly-minded who are most effective in their life on earth. Our 'death denying, live-forever-down-here culture' means we can be ill equipped to face our death or the death of a loved one at times.[38] Rather than

---

37 Ibid., p. 6.

38 I have borrowed this phrase from Packer, *A Grief Sanctified*, p. 147.

seeming morbid and death-obsessed, visions of our own mortality can help us use the time we have on earth most effectively to glorify our God.

Baxter knew that the best life was not to be found in the here and now. In a culture nowadays that centres itself on running after pleasure and running away from pain, Baxter proves a helpful balm. This life is not the pinnacle of our existence; the next one is. It is true that Baxter used joys in this world to help him vividly imagine the next, but he also knew that 'God's servants have not their portion or good things in this life.'[39] The best life cannot and will not be found in this one, but instead is to be found in the next, when we shall experience perfection in us, perfection in others, and will rejoice forever in the glorious presence of our Lord.

We finish with a poem by Baxter, *The Covenant and Confidence of Faith*. It was an encouragement to his dear wife, as she copied it out for her own personal reflection. May it encourage us too to think and act in such as way as to show we believe heaven to be our future reality.

Now it belongs not to my care
Whether I die or live:
To love and serve you is my share,
And this your grace must give.
If life be long, I will be glad,
That I may long obey:
If short, yet why should I be sad,
That shall have the same pay?

---

39 Ibid., p. 165.

Christ leads me through no darker rooms
Than he went through before;
He that into God's kingdom comes
Must enter by this door.
Come, Lord, when grace has made me meet
Your blessed face to see;
For if your work on earth be sweet,
What will your glory be?

Then I shall end my sad complaints
And weary sinful days,
And join with the triumphant saints
That sing Jehovah's praise.
My knowledge of that life is small;
The eye of faith is dim;
But it's enough that Christ knows all,
And I shall be with him.[40]

For further reading:

Packer, J. I., *A Quest for Godliness: The Puritan Vision of the Christian Life* (Wheaton, IL.: Crossway Books, 1990).

For the adventurous:

Baxter, Richard, *The Reformed Pastor*. Edited by Hugh Martin (London: SCM Press, 1956).

Baxter, Richard and Benjamin Fawcett, *The Saints' Everlasting Rest* (Grand Rapids, MI: Baker Book House, 1978).

---

40 Ibid., pp. 138-9.

John Wesley
A Brand Plucked from the Burning

IAN J. MADDOCK

It was late at night and the Epworth rectory was burning. The fire that had begun only shortly beforehand was now rapidly threatening to engulf the entire house. The local minister, Samuel Wesley, had swiftly managed to gather as many of his sizable household as he could—himself, his pregnant wife Susanna, their maid, and all of their eight children (or so he hoped)—and lead them to the safety of the garden. Once they were outside they conducted a headcount, only to discover aghast that one child was missing—none other than five-year-old John. There being no way now to reach him (Samuel's brave efforts to rescue any stragglers on the upper floor ended when the burning staircase collapsed under his weight), all the remaining family members could do was to kneel in prayer and commit young John's life to God.

Meanwhile, amidst the commotion and fast approaching danger, John Wesley was still in bed asleep! His recollections of the night of Thursday, February 9, 1709 ('I remember all the circumstances as distinctly as though it were but yesterday') was that neither the heat nor smoke was enough to rouse him, but instead the bright light of the encroaching inferno—he thought dawn had arrived early! When the maid failed to answer his call, John put his 'head out of the curtains and saw streaks of fire on top of the room.' Wesley had the presence of mind to climb on top of a chest near the window, where he was spotted by neighbours who immediately rallied to his aid. Some men constructed a human ladder and helped him down just in the nick of time before the roof fell in. 'So by the infinite mercy of almighty God,' reflected his mother, 'our lives were well preserved by little less than [a] miracle, for there passed but a few moments between the first discovery of the fire and the falling of the house.'[1]

Following John's close shave, Susanna would go on to famously describe him as 'a brand plucked from the burning,' echoing the words of Zechariah 3:2. In the process she instilled in her son's life an early sense of providential destiny—an awareness that his life had been saved, not simply *from* an untimely death, but *for* the purpose of achieving great things in God's service. Wesley embraced this event as a defining moment and

---

1   Charles Wallace Jr (ed.), *Susanna Wesley: The Complete Writings* (New York: Oxford, 1997), p. 67.

this verse as a virtual motto. For instance, George Vertue's 1741 portrait of Wesley not only features a drawing of his dramatic rescue some three decades earlier, but also the inscription 'Is not this a Brand pluck'd out of the Fire?' Likewise, in the midst of a serious illness in 1753 from which he feared he wouldn't recover, Wesley included the words of Zechariah 3:2 in an inscription he commissioned for his own tombstone (his fears of an imminent demise proved premature; he would go on to live another thirty-eight years!).

John Wesley would become one of the most recognizable Englishmen during the eighteenth century, a leader of what became known as the evangelical revival that transformed Great Britain's religious landscape (the revivals that broke out on the other side of the Atlantic were referred to as the 'Great Awakening'). And yet his route from the relative obscurity of Lincolnshire to the undisputed figurehead of a movement that became known as 'Methodism' was a circuitous one.

From Epworth to Oxford

Wesley was born on June 28, 1703, the fifteenth (approximately—the precise numbers are a little hazy!) of eighteen children born to Samuel and Susanna Wesley. Only eleven survived infancy, including John's younger brother Charles, who would go on to become a prolific and famous hymn writer. His home life was shaped by his father's affinity for High-Church Anglicanism and his mother's fondness for strict Puritan discipline ('Break the will, if you will not damn the child' was how she summarised her philosophy of parenthood). In time, Wesley would come to embody a fusion of his father's bookishness and his mother's focus on practical theology. Some have described him as a 'folk-theologian.'

Up until the age of ten, Wesley was home schooled and discouraged from mixing with local Epworth children. All that was to change in 1714 when he was thrust out of these cloistered environs and arrived at the Charterhouse school as a boarder, the recipient of a scholarship for needy students (Wesley's father was in perennial financial trouble, even to the point of spending time in 'debtors prison' in 1705). University studies followed at Christ Church, Oxford. Wesley graduated with a BA in 1724, remaining in Oxford as he fulfilled the remaining requirements for his Masters degree.

Like many before and after him, it was around this point in his life that Wesley began to seriously consider his vocational options and along with it his very sense of personal and spiritual identity. A career in higher education was one possibility—Wesley was elected a Fellow of Lincoln College, Oxford, in 1726, much to his parents' delight. Another course, and not mutually exclusive with the former, was to follow in his father's and older brother's footsteps and pursue ordination in the Church of England. While there was curiously little expectation during this period that prospective clergy feel a strong sense of vocational call, Wesley sensed that this was not a decision to be taken lightly. Throughout 1725 he corresponded regularly with his mother, who not only encouraged him to seek ordination but also helped him solidify what would become some of his most cherished and distinctive theological commitments, especially his lifelong allergic reaction to Calvinism's doctrine of unconditional election and his lifelong focus on holiness as the essence of true Christianity.[2]

Holiness

A relentless pursuit of holiness came to define Wesley's life. He devoured Thomas á Kempis' *Of the Imitation of Christ*, Jeremy Taylor's *Rules and Exercises of Holy Living and Holy Dying* and William Law's *A Treatise on Christian Perfection* and *A Serious Call to a Devout and Holy Life*. This reading diet rubbed off. Outwardly, his quest for holiness expressed itself in terms of austerity, discipline and religious zeal. Inwardly, though, Wesley yearned for a deeper holiness, 'a renewal of soul in the image of God ... a complex habit of lowliness, meekness, purity, faith, hope and love of God and man.'[3] A poignant example of his unrelenting spiritual introspection was a diary he kept where he tried to measure the fervency of his holiness hour by hour. Not only did Wesley pursue holiness for himself, but ever

---

2   Ralph Waller, *John Wesley: A Personal Portrait* (London: SPCK, 2003) pp. 22-3.

3   Frank Baker (ed.), *Letters I-II*. Works of John Wesley: Bicentennial Edition 25-26 (Nashville, TN: Abingdon, 1980-1982) 25:399.

and always the mentor, he encouraged eager acolytes to do likewise. They became known pejoratively as the Holy Club—the original Methodists—and included among their alumni the soon-to-be celebrity evangelist George Whitefield.

Wesley might well have been thoroughly converted to holiness during his years at Oxford, but was it a conversion in an evangelical sense? Wesley himself seems to suggest not. In fact, in retrospect he recognised that he hadn't truly come to understand the grace that lies at the heart of the gospel and was effectively trying to earn his way into heaven. He wrote, 'by my continued *endeavour to keep his whole law*, inward and outward, *to the utmost of my power*, I was persuaded that I should be accepted of him.'[4] His hope was that God would overlook his shortcomings and instead look approvingly on his religious sincerity. He reflected afterwards, 'I was ordained Deacon in 1725, and Priest in the year following. But it was many years after this before I was convinced of the great truths above recited. During all that time I was utterly ignorant of the nature and condition of justification. Sometimes I confounded it with sanctification ...'[5]

---

4   W. Reginald Ward and Richard P. Heitzenrater (eds.), *Journals and Diaries I-VII*. Works of John Wesley: Bicentennial Edition 19-24 (Nashville, TN: Abingdon, 1988-1997), 18:244-5.

5   Thomas Jackson (ed.), *The Works of John Wesley*. 14 Volumes (Kansas City, MO: Beacon Hill, 1979), 8:111.

'I felt my heart strangely warmed'

Wesley's so-called 'Aldersgate Street experience'—what we might call his second conversion—was a dramatic turning point in this respect. While his visceral experience of God's forgiveness that evening didn't displace holiness from the centre of his theology, it was the point at which he came to realise that we need to be justified before we can be sanctified—not the other way around. Wesley had only recently arrived back in London after a two-year expedition as a missionary with the Society for the Propagation of the Gospel in Savannah, Georgia. This failed adventure had come to an abrupt and ignominious end. He failed to arrive at the sense of assurance he saw so joyfully expressed by Moravian missionaries (especially in the midst of a life-threatening storm as they crossed the Atlantic together in 1736). He also failed miserably in his efforts to evangelise the Native American population ('I went to America to convert the Indians; but oh! Who shall convert me?'[6]). He did succeed, however, in fleeing Savannah under the cover of darkness in December 1737, with a defamation trial against him still pending after a relationship with the chief magistrate's niece turned sour![7]

---

6   Ward and Heitzenrater (eds.), *Journals and Diaries*, 18:211.

7   Stephen Tomkins, *John Wesley: A Biography* (Grand Rapids, IL: Eerdmans, 2003), pp. 51-5.

Short on confidence—of his standing before God, let alone what he should do next—Wesley's encounter with another Moravian missionary, Peter Böhler, would prove to be instrumental. 'The faith I want,' longed Wesley, 'is "a sure trust and confidence in God, that through the merits of Christ my sins are forgiven, and I am reconciled to the favour of God."' Böhler offered some curious advice: 'Preach faith until you have it; and then, because you have it, you will preach faith.'[8]

This is exactly what Wesley did, and it's eventually what happened. His brother Charles had just experienced the new birth a few days before, when on May 24, 1738, John Wesley went to a Moravian gathering at Aldersgate Street in London where they were reading the Preface to Luther's commentary on Romans. Wesley's description of what happened next has become enshrined in evangelical folklore:

> About a quarter before nine, while he was describing the change which God works in the heart through faith in Christ, I felt my heart strangely warmed. I felt I did trust in Christ, Christ alone for salvation; and an assurance was given me that He had taken away *my* sins, even *mine*, and saved *me* from the law of sin and death.[9]

---

8   Ward and Heitzenrater (eds.), *Journals and Diaries*, 18:228.

9   Ibid., 18:249-50.

An itinerant field-preacher of one book

And yet as formative as these first and second conversions were in Wesley's life, it was another, third, conversion that set him on the path towards becoming the 'John Wesley' who was so widely known during his own lifetime and is still remembered today. Here we're referring to the way Wesley controversially embraced itinerant field-preaching as a key part of his effort to reach vast segments of socio-economically—and spiritually—marginalised British society with the gospel. Even more, he would go on to resource and oversee an army of fellow itinerant field-preachers to aide in this endeavour.

Wesley was many things at once: author, editor, translator, hymnist, amateur physician (his *Primitive Physic* is still in print), teacher and organiser. But above all else, he was a preacher. If his highest ambition was to be *homo unius libri* (a man of one book), then his life was spent living out that desire as a preacher of one book—and more particularly, as an *itinerant field*-preacher of one book. Many of his public portraits memorialise this self-identity. For example, Nathaniel Hone (1766) and John Russell (1773) both depict Wesley as a field-preacher of one book; preaching in a rustic setting, his right hand raised (but not too high, modelling his instructions to Methodist preachers that they ought to extend their arms no more than a foot from their body!) and the other holding a Bible (one finger marking a page, sending the clear message that the Bible was no mere prop in his sermons).

While Wesley's peripatetic lifestyle would slow as his years advanced, he was still preaching two weeks before his death on March 2, 1791, aged eighty-seven. Over the previous five decades he travelled over 250,000 miles (in all weather, often on horseback) preaching an estimated 40,000 sermons. If Wesley's candid assessment was that his compatriot George Whitefield was prematurely aged by field-preaching—that he preached himself to death—then his own experience was that he preached to live! As he got older, Wesley's habit was to describe the state of his health in his Journal (in terms of genre, this was less a 'dear diary' and more literature intended to edify Methodist Societies). Wesley attributed his good health, not so much to his diet, but instead to the invigorating effects of a busy preaching schedule! For instance, on his seventy-seventh birthday he wrote, 'I can hardly think I am entering this day into the seventy-eighth year of my age. By the blessing of God I am just the same as when I entered the twenty-eighth. This hath God wrought, chiefly by my constant exercise, my rising early, and preaching morning and evening.' Two years later and he was still defying chronological gravity: 'I find no more pain or bodily infirmities than at five and twenty. This I still impute... to my constant preaching, particularly in the morning.'[10]

Given Wesley's temperament and upbringing (as he once put it, 'I'm a High-Churchman, the son of a High-

10 Ibid., 23:179-80, pp. 244-5.

Churchman'), the fact that he even considered what he styled 'this strange way of preaching in the fields'—of preaching anywhere that wasn't consecrated ground for that matter—was a monumental step. By contrast, when Whitefield began field-preaching in February 1739 in England's west country, his conscience seemingly unencumbered by any ecclesiological qualms, he took to it like a duck to water. His dramatic oratory, when added to the sheer novelty value, made him an immediate sensation. Pretty soon he found himself in high demand. Whitefield couldn't be everywhere at once and so he enlisted Wesley's help, advertising that his mentor would be preaching in his place in Bristol in early April—and only then letting Wesley know after the fact![11]

As far as Wesley was concerned, the whole matter was scandalous; not simply the way he'd been conscripted into action, but even more the activity he had been conscripted into. After watching Whitefield preach outdoors in late March, 1739 he reflected, 'I had been all my life (till very lately) so tenacious of every point relating to decency and order that I should have thought the saving of souls almost a sin if it had not been done in a church.'[12] And yet Wesley caught the same expansive evangelistic vision that had so captivated Whitefield. The Church of England's parish system hadn't kept up with

---

11 Joel Houston, '"Beginning a Society of Their Own": John Wesley, George Whitefield and the Bristol Division' in Ian J. Maddock (ed.), *Wesley and Whitefield? Wesley versus Whitefield?* (Eugene, OR: Pickwick, 2018) p. 12.

12 Ward and Heitzenrater (eds.), *Journals and Diaries*, 19:46.

rapid urbanization, especially in coal mining regions in England's west and north. Who will reach the unreached?

Wesley became convicted that unless somebody went and preached to the largely illiterate and unchurched—and in a way they could understand—there was little prospect of many of them ever hearing the gospel. Justifying his decision to defy his superiors and pursue an itinerant field-preaching ministry, Wesley asked, 'What is the end of all ecclesiastical order?'

> Is it not to bring souls from the power of Satan unto God? ... Now I would fain know, where has order answered these ends? Not in any place where I have been: not among the tinners in Cornwall, the keelmen at Newcastle, the colliers in Kingswood and Staffordshire; not among the drunkards, swearers, Sabbath-breakers of Moorfields, or the harlots of Drury Lane.[13]

It's almost as though Wesley hears God speak to him, 'It's too small a thing for you to be a light to Oxford.' Fusing Apostolic Christianity and Enlightenment bravado, he famously declared 'the whole world is now my parish,' and on April 2, 1739 proceeded to preach his very own sermon on the mount. His description of this event is not only full of pathos, but also a palpable sense of realised destiny. *This* was the vocation he'd been preserved by God to fulfil:

---

13   Baker (ed.), *Letters*, 26:206.

> At four in the afternoon I submitted to be more vile, and proclaimed in the highways the glad tidings of salvation, speaking from a little eminence in a ground adjoining to the city, to about three thousand people. The scripture on which I spoke was this... 'The Spirit of the Lord is upon Me, because he hath anointed me to preach the gospel to the poor. He hath sent Me to heal the broken-hearted; to preach deliverance to the captives, and recovery of sight to the blind; to set at liberty them that are bruised, to proclaim the acceptable year of the Lord.'[14]

These were drastic times, and Wesley felt that they called for drastic, unorthodox measures. Rationalizing his efforts to proactively take the gospel to coal-miners and their families—and not expect them to come to him—he reasoned, 'Had the minister of the parish preached like an angel, it had profited them nothing; for they heard him not.' And so he was quite prepared to exploit the novelty value of field-preaching, if that's what it took: 'But when one came and said, "Yonder is a man preaching on top of a mountain," they ran in droves to hear what he would say.' The ends justified the means: 'Had it not been for field preaching, the uncommonness of which was the very circumstances that recommended it, they must have run on in the error of their way, and perished in their blood.'[15]

---

14 Ward and Heitzenrater (eds.), *Journals and Diaries*, 19:42.

15 Gerald R. Cragg (ed.), *The Appeals to Men of Reason and Religion and Certain Related Open Letters*. Works of John Wesley:

People's eternal destiny was at stake—and not just his hearers, but his own! Wesley feared that if he didn't continue in the path he'd set out on, he would risk forfeiting his own salvation. 'But you know no call I have to preach up and down, to play the part of an itinerant evangelist,' he wrote to one critic. 'But I do; I know God hath required this at my hands... that were I to refrain I should never hear that word "Well done, good and faithful servant," but "Cast ye the unprofitable servant into outer darkness, where there is weeping and gnashing of teeth".'[16]

But if Wesley was a stubbornly convinced field-preacher, there's also a sense in which he was a reluctant field-preacher. Whereas Whitefield was right in his element, Wesley had to force himself to become a field-preacher in spite of his natural inclinations. He made it very clear that if he had his way, he'd much prefer to be back in Oxford, 'a wanderer in the academic groves' and a 'philosophical sluggard.'[17] Whereas Whitefield presented a relatively romanticised view of the itinerant lifestyle (his published Journals often read as a gripping adventure travelogue), Wesley's descriptions are much earthier. Field-preaching was a cross to bear: 'What a marvel the devil does not love field-preaching,' he wrote in 1759. 'Neither do I: I love a commodious room, a soft cushion, a handsome pulpit. But where is my zeal, if I do

Bicentennial Edition 11 (Nashville, TN: Abingdon, 1989) 11:306-7.

16 Baker (ed.), *Letters*, 26:237.

17 Ibid., 26:197.

not trample all these underfoot in order to save one more soul.'[18] To one of his many detractors who queried the propriety of field-preaching, Wesley asked:

Let me ask you one plain question: 'For what gain (setting conscience aside) will *you* be obliged to act thus? To live exactly as I do? For what price will *you* preach (and that with all your might, not in an easy, indolent fashionable way) eighteen or nineteen times every week? And this throughout the year? What shall I give *you* to travel seven or eight hundred miles, in all weathers, every two or three months. For what salary will *you* abstain from all other diversions than the doing good and praising God? I am mistaken if you would not prefer strangling to such a life, even with thousands of gold and silver.[19]

Wesley became a keen student of the 'science' of open-air public speaking. He sought out natural amphitheatres from which he could best amplify his voice. He utilised walls and coal pits as sounding boards. Makeshift pulpits came in many guises. He once famously said he did more good preaching standing on top of his father's tombstone in Epworth than he did preaching for three years from his pulpit!

In order to be understood by those less privileged with the upbringing and education he had received, Wesley even intentionally went about reinventing the way he

18 Ward and Heitzenrater (eds.), *Journals and Diaries*, 21:203.
19 Cragg (ed.), *Appeals*, 11:86.

communicated. He cut out long sentences and multi-syllabic words from his vocabulary as part of his effort to preach 'plain truth to plain people.' On one occasion, a friend from his Oxford days, Samuel Furley, approached Wesley for advice about how best to follow in his ministry footsteps. Hear Wesley's homiletical advice: 'Clearness in particular is necessary for you and me, because we are to instruct people of the lowest understanding. Therefore we, above all, if we think with the wise, yet must speak with the vulgar. We should constantly use the most common, little, easy words which our language affords.' Wesley had learned this lesson the hard way! 'When I had been a member of the University about ten years, I wrote and talked much as you do now. But when I talked to plain people in the Castle or the town, they gaped and stared. This quickly obliged me to alter my style and adopt the language of those I spoke to.' In Wesley, the imperative to evangelise merged with a spirit of *noblesse oblige*—or the responsibilities that came with privilege:

> And yet there is dignity in this simplicity, which is not disagreeable to those of the highest rank... You are a Christian minister, speaking and writing to save souls. Have this end always in your eye, and you will never designedly use a hard word. Use all the sense, learning and fire you have, forgetting yourself, and remembering only that these are the souls for whom Christ died.[20]

---

20 John Telford (ed.), *The Letters of the Rev. John Wesley*. 8 vols. (London: Epworth, 1931), 4:257-8.

Sometimes we can get the impression that because Wesley was an itinerant field-preacher he spent his time travelling about helter-skelter. And yet nothing was further from the truth. He was highly strategic, establishing a widespread network of preaching 'circuits,' each serviced by a number of itinerant preachers. Ever the mentor (and as the movement's undisputed figurehead), Wesley was fond of making detailed and practical lists of rules aimed at eliminating a range of potential faux pas among his preachers, many of whom barely had the equivalent of a high school education, let alone formal theological training. He was concerned with the whole homiletical package: not just *what* was preached ('Take care not to ramble from your text, but keep close to it'; 'Beware of allegorizing or spiritualizing too much'), but also *how* and *when* it was preached ('Take care of anything awkward or affected, either in your gesture or your pronunciation'; when reciting the Lord's prayer, remember that it's 'Hallowed, not hollowed be your name'; 'Be Punctual!').[21]

Sowing *and* Watering

And yet as important as preaching was for Wesley, it wasn't the sum total of his ministry. Whereas fellow Methodist field-preacher George Whitefield envisaged his

---

21 Henry D. Rack (ed.), *The Methodist Societies: The Minutes of Conference*. Works of John Wesley: Bicentennial Edition 10 (Nashville, TN: Abingdon, 2011), 10:207.

ministry more or less exclusively in terms of preaching—and evangelistic preaching in particular—Wesley was committed to supplementing his evangelistic preaching with deliberate ongoing discipleship. It wasn't enough to simply 'sow' God's Word; it needed to be 'watered' too.

The stereotype goes that wherever Whitefield went he left an overwhelming impression of impassioned eloquence, but wherever Wesley went he left a Methodist Society. These Societies (further subdivided into Classes and Bands—concentric circles of ever-increasing piety) were first established in the 1740s and grew dramatically under Wesley's leadership. From small beginnings in Oxford, by the time of his death in 1791 it's estimated that there were 72,000 members across the British Isles, including Ireland. In 1784, after the Bishop of London refused to ordain any Methodist preachers serving in the American colonies, Wesley took the unprecedented step of ordaining Thomas Coke to serve as the Superintendent of the newly formed Methodist Episcopal Church. Although Wesley's stated ambition was always to help reform the Church of England—not create a rival denomination—this is ultimately what eventuated in 1795.

At first—though always in Wesley's heart—Methodism was a working-class movement. He intentionally established Methodist bases in cities like London, Newcastle and Bristol; growing urban centres with an even faster expanding economic underclass. 'I bear the rich, and love the poor, therefore I spend all my time with them,' he once wrote.[22] In a society that often equated poverty with moral impoverishment, Wesley offered a compassionate counter-voice. In 1753, reflecting on the plight of the working poor, he declared, 'So wickedly, so devilishly false, is that common objection: "they are poor because they are idle".'[23]

The Methodists quickly became known for their care for people's spiritual *and* physical welfare. Wesley established a medical dispensary at his London base (The Foundery), schools in London and Kingswood, and a Poorhouse that consciously sought to live out the Apostle James' exhortation to practice a religion that is 'pure and undefiled' by providing housing for orphans and widows. Wesley not only had a heart for the impoverished, but also the oppressed. His last letter, written on February 24, 1791, was to none other than the abolitionist William Wilberforce, urging him on 'in opposing that execrable villainy, which is the scandal of religion, of England, and of human nature.' Wesley's encouragement is both realistic and prophetic:

> Unless God has raised you up for this very thing, you will be worn out by the opposition of men and devils. But if God be for you, who can be against you? Are all of them together stronger than God? O be not weary of well-doing! Go on, in the name of God and in the power of His might, till even American slavery

---

22 Ted A. Campbell (ed.), *Letters III*. Works of John Wesley: Bicentennial Edition 27 (Nashville, TN: Abingdon, 2015), 27:391.

23 Ward and Heitzenrater (eds.), *Journals and Diaries*, 20:445.

(the vilest that ever saw the sun) shall vanish away before it.[24]

But as the Methodists grew in number they also changed socially and demographically. Socio-economically, they became more upwardly mobile, so much so that as time went on Wesley became alarmed that his people were increasingly losing touch with their roots. Towards the end of his life, he produced a flurry of sermons warning the Methodists of the seductions of wealth: 'On Dress' (1786), 'The Dangers of Riches' (1788), 'On Worldly Folly' and 'The Dangers of Increasing Riches' (1790). Despite earning a significant income through his published writings, Wesley achieved his ambition to die with no wealth that anyone could inherit. He didn't simply preach 'earn all you can, save all you can, and give all you can'[25]—he practiced it too.

Wesley's Legacy

In this chapter we've painted a largely rosy picture of John Wesley. The reality was that, like all of us, he was full of contradictions. Though he preached the possibility of Christian perfection, he was a work in progress. Wesley had an unfortunate habit of caricaturing Calvinism

---

24 Quoted in Henry Moore, *The Life of John Wesley*. 2 vols. (New York: Methodist Episcopal Church, 1826), 2:257.

25 See Wesley's sermon 'The Use of Money' in Albert C. Outler (ed.), *Sermons*. Works of John Wesley: Bicentennial Edition 1-4 (Nashville: Abingdon, 1984-1987), 2:263-280.

and slandering Calvinists (Whitefield excepted!). His marriage was a shambles and ended in separation; he only learned of his wife's death after she had been buried. He had a reputation for being autocratic and imperious. No one person succeeded Wesley as the leader of Methodism, and that by his own design.

And yet, while Wesley was undoubtedly a driven and ambitious man, he was also profoundly humble— the sort of humility that accompanies a deep awareness that it's by grace alone that we are saved. He embraced the Apostle Paul's vision and was prepared to become all things to all people in order to win some, even if that meant letting go of prestige, status and comfort. God gave him eyes to see that there's a mission field right on his own doorstep and that as disciples of Jesus we can cross cultures without leaving our own postcode. As one of evangelicalism's founding fathers, John Wesley is an encouragement for us to go and do likewise.

For further reading

S. Tomkins, *John Wesley: A Biography* (Grand Rapids, MI: Eerdmans, 2003).

R. Waller, *John Wesley: A Personal Portrait* (London: SPCK, 2003).

For the adventurous

H. Rack, *Reasonable Enthusiast* (Peterborough: Epworth, 2002).

Hudson Taylor
Those I Must Bring Also

RACHEL CIANO

A brush with death

Hudson Taylor, born in 1832 in South Yorkshire, England, was sure of two things from early on in his life: that he wanted to do ministry in China, and that God would provide for that ministry if that was indeed where God wanted him. While training as a medical student in preparation for heading to China, Taylor had a very close encounter with death. He was sewing together some sheets of paper in order to take lecture notes on them, and in doing so, accidentally pricked his finger with the sewing needle. The next day at the hospital, he was dissecting the body of a person who had died of a terrible fever. Taylor and his fellow students knew that in dissecting such a body, the smallest scratch could allow infection to enter their bodies and cost them their lives. He was certainly careful not to scratch himself in the procedure. He had, however, forgotten about the finger-prick from the night before.

As the day progressed, Taylor became more and more unwell. His supervisor advised him to take a hansom cab (a kind of horse-drawn carriage) home immediately, so he could arrange his affairs, telling Taylor, 'you are a dead man.'[1] Taylor was at first full of sorrow that he would therefore not be going to China. Before long, however, he became convinced by the feeling that 'unless I am greatly mistaken, I have work to do in China, and shall not die.'[2] He struggled home on foot, and when he became too weak to walk, took a bus (he didn't have enough money to take a hansom cab!). He finally made it home, where he soon collapsed unconscious. A long period of recovery followed (the visiting doctor prescribed port and lamb chops daily), and after several weeks he was well enough to leave his room. Two other men had died of dissection wounds they received at the same time as Taylor, while Taylor said he was 'spared in answer to prayer to work for God in China.'[3]

Taylor had a very real and deep sense that God would provide for gospel work amongst the millions in China, and that God would never forsake him, even in the darkest times. This belief grew and matured at

---

1   J. Hudson Taylor, *Hudson Taylor's Spiritual Pilgrimage (Formerly 'a Retrospect')*: *An Autobiography of the Founder of the China Inland Mission* (Melbourne: China Inland Mission), p. 32.

2   Ibid.

3   Ibid., p. 34.

different stages of his life, but it was, nonetheless, a common feature throughout his life. He exercised this conviction during the numerous challenges in his life—his and his family's health and well-being, finances and workers for the task, testing new ministry strategies and methods. Life was certainly not easy for Taylor; indeed, for much of it, it was full of difficulties and heartache. Yet, near the end of his life, looking back at where God had taken him, he wrote, 'Go forward in the strength of the Lord, and in the sufficiency that comes from Him alone...and thank Him for your conscious insufficiency, for when you are weak, then He can be strong in you.'[4]

Trusting God to get him to China

China captured Hudson's heart and mind from very early in his life. When he was a newborn baby his parents prayed that he would be a missionary to China, an area of increasing interest for mission, owing in large part to Britain's colonial interests there. The prayer of parents can be powerful and effective! He was converted at the age of seventeen after reading an evangelistic pamphlet, and soon after was asking God to give him some work to do for Him as 'an outlet for love and gratitude; some self-denying service, no matter what it might be, however trying or however trivial; something with which He would

---

4   Taylor wrote this in 1898, from Kuling (now Guling), a new mission station in lush hills in China. Quoted in Dr and Mrs Howard Taylor, *Biography of James Hudson Taylor* (London: Hodder and Stoughton, 1973), p. 492.

be pleased, and that I might do for Him who had done so much for me.'[5] He said he put himself, his life, his friends, his all, upon the altar, lying 'silent before Him with unspeakable awe and unspeakable joy.'[6] Hudson Taylor made a resolution to serve God with all his heart and soul as a teenager, not knowing where that would lead him, but trusting his God who went before him. You can never be too young to be serious about the Lord.

Taylor anticipated the danger of mission work in China, writing, 'it seemed to me highly probable that the work to which I was thus called might cost my life.'[7] He borrowed a book from a local minister on China, and when asked why, he responded that 'God had called me to spend my life in missionary service in that land.'[8] The minister asked him about his plan to get there, and Taylor replied he didn't know, but probably like those sent out by Jesus in the Gospels without money or means, 'relying on Him who had called me to supply all my need.'[9] The minister kindly placed his hand on Taylor's shoulder, and replied, 'Ah, my boy, as you grow older you will get wiser than that. Such an idea would do very well in the days when Christ Himself was on earth, but not now.'[10] Taylor, who recounts this incident in his

5   Taylor, p. 11.
6   Ibid., p. 12.
7   Ibid.
8   Ibid.
9   Ibid.
10   Ibid., pp. 12-13.

Retrospect, wrote, 'I have grown older since then, but not wiser,' knowing God always provides for the work He has directed.[11] 'If I *am* guided by God, in going out, He will open the way and provide the means.'[12]

Taylor made preparations to travel to China, studying medicine and Mandarin. He also continued the spiritual practices of attentive Bible reading and prayer that were to help sustain him in the hardship and heartache to come. Later, when on long and arduous travels into the inland regions of China, Taylor would write of the importance of devotional practices even when time poor, saying that the hardest part of being a missionary was maintaining regular, prayerful Bible study: 'Satan will always find you something to do, when you ought to be occupied about that, if it is only arranging a window blind.'[13] Hudson Taylor's son, Frederick, remembers travelling with his dad month after month in northern China. Stopping in inns at night to sleep, they would string up curtains for privacy from other travellers sleeping in the same, large room as them. Once everyone had fallen asleep, Hudson would light a match, and however tired, would pore over his Bible and pray. He found 2 a.m. to 4 a.m. the ideal time

11 Ibid., p. 13.

12 A. J. Broomhall, *Hudson Taylor & China's Open Century: Book Two: Over the Treaty Wall* (London: Hodder & Stoughton, 1982), p. 88. Emphasis original.

13 Howard Taylor and Howard Mrs Taylor, *Hudson Taylor's Spiritual Secret, Hendrickson Classic Biography* (Peabody, MA: Hendrickson Publishers, 2008), p. 201.

to be uninterrupted and so be able to devote himself to Bible reading and prayer.[14]

Taylor was an ordinary Christian using the ordinary ways that God uses to sustain the faith and spiritual health of His people—Bible reading and prayer. Hudson applied himself to healthy devotional practices in this way because he knew how much he needed it. He got incredibly frustrated and disheartened with his ungodliness, with his lack of progress in the Christian life. However, he knew prayer and Bible study were vital for God to grow him and change him. At seventy years of age he said to one of his children: 'I have just finished reading the Bible through, today, for the fortieth time in forty years.'[15] His son and daughter-in-law could write of him, 'he not only read it, but lived it' and 'that flicker of candlelight [where Hudson read the Bible at night] has meant more to them than all they have read or heard on secret [private] prayer; it meant reality, not preaching but practice.'[16]

On September 19, 1853 twenty-one-year-old Taylor boarded the small ship in Liverpool that was to carry him to China to work with the Chinese Evangelisation Society. His mother saw him off, and Hudson Taylor prayed with her and others moments before departure. His voice started to break when he committed to God those he loved, but he echoed the words of Paul's farewell to the

---

14 This is recounted in ibid., pp. 200-1.

15 Ibid., p. 202.

16 Ibid., pp. 201-2.

elders from Ephesus: 'But I do not account my life of any value nor as precious to myself, if only I may finish my course and the ministry that I received from the Lord Jesus, to testify to the gospel of the grace of God.' (Acts 20:24, ESV). Neither Hudson Taylor nor his mother thought they would see each other again on this earth and when she farewelled him, she sat down, shaking and crying on the dock. Even though this day had been anticipated for years, and had been prayed for by his parents, the cold, hard reality of the separation was still overwhelming. It is a cost not only to those who leave to serve the Lord away from home, but also a cost to those who remain at home without them. After an extremely rough and at times quite terrifying voyage, Taylor finally arrived on the shores of China on March 1, 1854, after five and a half months at sea. 'My feelings on stepping ashore I cannot attempt to describe. My heart felt as though it had not room and must burst its bonds, while tears of gratitude and thankfulness fell from my eyes.'[17]

Commencing work in China

Upon arriving in Shanghai Taylor became acquainted with missionaries working in the area. However, he soon grew frustrated with them. They laughed at or criticised his decision to dress in Chinese rather than European clothing. Taylor's costume change included Chinese spectacles and baggy pantaloons, and to add insult to

---

17 Howard Taylor and Howard Mrs Taylor, *Biography of James Hudson Taylor* (London: China Inland Mission, 1965), p. 92.

injury, he also dared to wear his hair as Chinese men did, dying it black, and wearing it in a long pigtail (a clip-on one sometimes!).

Taylor was impatient with the existing missionaries for their lack of work inland. They were largely confined to the coast of China—little work had been done to reach the unreached interior of China, which is where Taylor's heart particularly lay. He also thought the missionaries, who were language specialists fluent in Mandarin, spent too much time as the translators for businessmen or diplomats. As the cost of living in Shanghai was high, and salaries from mission societies often low, the temptation to supplement their income this way meant that they often neglected their missionary work. Nonetheless, Taylor considered them 'worldly' and neglectful of their God-given duties.

Taylor eventually resigned from the Chinese Evangelisation Society, and set up a new ministry with a co-worker two hundred kilometres down the coast from Shanghai, in Ningbo. It was here that he was to meet his future wife, Maria Dyer. Hudson Taylor was not considered suitable for Maria—he didn't have a degree (he left England without completing his studies in medicine), he didn't have a mission society, he wasn't even ordained, and to make matters worse, he had the thoroughly eccentric practice of dressing like a Chinese person. Their romance triumphed in the end, and they married in January 1858, when Maria was twenty-one and Hudson twenty-five. Part of the daily pattern of married life was studying the Greek New Testament together before breakfast—they took the mantra, 'Bible before breakfast' to a whole new level!

After working tirelessly together for the next two years, Hudson's health took a turn for the worst. They were reluctant to leave the work and the people in China, with Hudson writing, 'it was no small trial to part from those whom we had learned so truly to love in the Lord', referring to their newly organised church of 30-40 locals.[18] It seemed to him 'a great calamity that failure of health compelled my relinquishing work for God in China, just when it was more fruitful than ever before; and to leave that little band of Christians in Ningbo, needing much care and teaching, was a great sorrow.'[19] Hudson believed that 'the only hope of restoration seemed to lie in a voyage to England and a brief stay in a more bracing climate,' and so they went back to London in 1860 with their baby Gracie, awaiting what the next chapter would hold.[20] The return to England was disappointing and painful as they left the work they had poured everything into, however this hiatus in England was to immensely further the work in China.

---

18 J. Hudson Taylor, *Hudson Taylor: The Autobiography of a Man Who Brought the Gospel to China*, Men of Faith (Minneapolis: Bethany House Publishers, 1987), p. 139.

19 Taylor, *Hudson Taylor's Spiritual Pilgrimage (Formerly 'a Retrospect')): An Autobiography of the Founder of the China Inland Mission*, pp. 117-18.

20 Taylor, *Hudson Taylor: The Autobiography of a Man Who Brought the Gospel to China*, p. 139.

Trusting God with all of China

So far, mission work in China had been limited to the eastern coastline. However, a treaty between the United Kingdom and China two decades before meant that foreigners were no longer confined to the coastal port areas. The vast interior of China was therefore open for missionaries to enter; however no mission agency had taken up the challenge yet. While Hudson was convalescing in England (and finishing his medical studies, and qualifying as a midwife—it seems he was someone who found it hard to sit still!), he began to be increasingly disturbed by this fact. He would later write that the thought of people in China dying without ever hearing the gospel kept him awake at night and gave him nightmares; at one point he even lamented of life itself because of this burden.

The major obstacle to ministry in the huge interior of China was the lack of willing workers. Taylor had prayed earnestly while back in China that God would raise up workers for the harvest, and even wrote to relatives in England, 'Do you know any earnest, devoted young men desirous of serving God in China...Oh, for four or five such helpers!'[21] However, no one came to help. In raising up workers for the vast harvest field of inland China, Hudson would again demonstrate his reliance on God to provide what He believed was needed for the work.

---

21 Ibid., pp. 138-9.

In 1865, five years into his recovery back in England, the opportunity came up for Hudson to spend some time on the south coast with a friend, in the seaside resort of Brighton. This was still the age of 'taking the waters'—the belief that sea bathing could cure almost any ailment, and Brighton was a popular spot to do it. However, Hudson was to receive a renewal of a different sort on the beach that Sunday morning. He had gone along to church, but he found all those people rejoicing in God overwhelming, given how he was so downcast. For the past few months he had been sleeping only an hour or so here and there, tormented by the thoughts that 'a million a month were dying without God' in China.[22] God made clear to him in that moment, 'other sheep I have…[those in China] those I must also bring.'[23] He suddenly came to the deep conviction and realisation that:

> If we are obeying the Lord, the responsibility rests *with Him*, not with us! … *You*, Lord, shall have all the burden! At Your bidding, as your servant I go forward, leaving results with You.[24]

He then asked God for two evangelists for each of the eleven unreached provinces, and two for the Mongolia/Tibet region. He opened his Bible and recorded the

---

22 Taylor and Taylor, *Biography of James Hudson Taylor*, p. 235.

23 Taylor and Taylor, *Hudson Taylor's Spiritual Secret*, p. 89.

24 Taylor and Taylor, *Biography of James Hudson Taylor*, p. 236. Emphasis original. Language updated for clarity.

simple, now famous words: 'Prayed for twenty-four willing skilful labourers at Brighton, June 25, 1865.'[25] First thing the next morning, he headed back to London. The day after, he wrote in his journal that he went to the bank and opened an account for the 'China Inland Mission' (CIM), depositing all he had (£10, around £11,000 today).[26] This is the first occurrence of the name of the mission that would shape his life from here on, and would define his legacy. In his prayers, and with his funds, he was trusting God with all of China, and now awaited God to answer.

The Taylors' house in London soon began to fill up with candidates for CIM, and the Saturday morning prayer meetings packed out the large house. The initial £10 grew into hundreds of pounds—all without asking people, only God. Following the pattern of his friend, George Müller, who ran an orphanage on the same principle, Hudson Taylor vowed to never ask people directly to supply their needs, but to ask God in prayer to work in people to compel them to give to the mission. 'Faith missions' were largely unheard of at the time, but it was to be a key characteristic of CIM.[27] Hudson Taylor

---

25 Ibid.

26 *Hudson Taylor's Spiritual Pilgrimage*, p. 94.

27 CIM eventually became today's Overseas Missionary Fellowship (OMF International) which continues to minister in East Asia, and maintains the same principle of not asking for financial support. People can, of course, give if they desire to but won't be asked directly. OMF today states, 'We believe God is able to supply our financial needs through His people and we pray regularly for his

had seen during his first stint in China God's provision of physical needs in quite dramatic, astounding ways—on the seas, in the face of violent attacks, in the face of sickness and expected death.[28] He had also seen the gross mishandling of resources and money during that time: 'money wrongly placed and money given for the wrong motives are both greatly to be dreaded.'[29] He argued that if people could not trust God to provide for their needs, it would be better for them to not go to China:

God owns all the gold and silver in the world, and the cattle on a thousand hills. We need not be vegetarians! We might indeed have had a guarantee fund if we had wished it; but we felt it was unnecessary and would do harm…We do not expect [God] to send three million missionaries to China, but if he did he would have ample means to sustain them all. Let us see that we keep God before our eyes; that we walk in his ways and seek to please and glorify him in everything, great and small. Depend upon it, God's work, done in God's way, will never lack God's supplies.[30]

provision. Our part, in the words of the Lord Jesus, is to "seek first His Kingdom and His righteousness."' https://omf.org/australia/support/ Accessed 19/02/2019.

28 The details of these hair-raising adventures can be found in Howard Taylor and Howard Mrs Taylor, *Hudson Taylor in Early Years: The Growth of a Soul* (London: China Inland Mission, 1911), pp. 429-92.

29 Taylor and Taylor, *Hudson Taylor's Spiritual Secret*, p. 97.

30 Ibid.

The vision becomes a reality

God raised up workers for the harvest field in what became known as the 'Lammermuir Party', named after the ship they sailed on. Amongst the eighteen adults there were nine single women. Single female missionaries were quite rare on the mission field in those days; however, women would have an integral part in the pioneering mission work with CIM. They would even run remote mission stations by themselves. The group set sail from London on May 26, 1866. It was a small ship and so travelled fast—the journey from London to Shanghai would take four months, rather than the usual six, arriving on September 30. It has been estimated that Hudson Taylor spent around five years of his life transiting about the world on a ship—it makes a long-haul flight look like a cake walk![31] On the sea journey, which was at times very perilous, many of the ship's crew were converted, pointing to the fact that these evangelists were always ready to share the gospel. Hudson Taylor's daughter, Gracie, also had a conversion experience on board after speaking with Jenny Faulding, one of the female missionaries (who would go on to marry Hudson Taylor after the death of Maria).

---

31 John Piper makes this estimate. See John Piper, *A Camaraderie of Confidence: The Fruit of Unfailing Faith in the Lives of Charles Spurgeon, George Muller, and Hudson Taylor, The Swans Are Not Silent* (Wheaton, IL: Crossway, 2016), p. 95.

The group pushed inland and upriver with the gospel. They arrived in Hangchow (now Hangzhou, approximately 200km southwest of Shanghai) in December 1866, and would spend the next sixteen months there. That time would be full of highs and lows. By the end of their time there there were fifty baptised Christians, many more people who were keen to hear the gospel, and a local pastor to help lead the church. However, that first year would also see the death of two members of the Lammermuir Party from smallpox, and the Taylors' daughter, Gracie, died of meningitis. Hudson poured out his heart in a letter to his mother:

> Is it possible that I shall nevermore feel the pressure of that little hand...nevermore see the sparkle of those bright eyes? And yet she is not lost...Pray for us. At times I seem almost overwhelmed with the internal and external trials connected with our work. But he has said, 'I will never leave you or forsake you,' and 'My strength is made perfect in weakness.' So be it.[32]

The group continued to press inland, and some members travelled by houseboat to the next place that may open to them. This continued to be the pattern for the missionaries. They dispersed further and further, establishing new work where they could, and then moving on to a new place to do it again. By the end of Hudson's life in 1905 there were 825 CIM missionaries

---

32 Taylor and Taylor, *Hudson Taylor's Spiritual Secret*, p. 112.

in all eighteen provinces of China, over 300 mission stations, more than 500 Chinese partners in ministry and 25,000 Chinese Christians.[33] God had grown His Church in China during Hudson's lifetime, and God continues to do so, despite co-ordinated attempts to thwart it. God may bury His messengers, but never His message.

Trusting God in the 'hardest year'[34]

A few years later, in 1870, Hudson Taylor was to experience one of the most difficult years of his life. In January their six-year-old son, Samuel, died of tuberculosis. Six months later on July 20, their thirteen day-old son, Noel, died (perhaps from cholera), and was buried next to his brother. Maria's health continued to worsen, and soon it was clear her tuberculosis enteritis (tuberculosis affecting the digestive system) would claim her life. She died three days after Noel, on July 23. She was thirty-three, and left behind Hudson and four surviving children.

Maria was certain she would meet Jesus at death but lamented leaving her husband. As she was dying, she said to him, 'I am not sorry to go to Him. But I am sorry to

---

33 Piper, pp. 95-6.

34 A. J. Broomhall, *Hudson Taylor & China's Open Century: Book Five: Refiner's Fire* (London: Hodder & Stoughton, 1985). 'The hardest year: 1870' is the title of this chapter in this book, and is an apt description of that year.

leave you alone at this time.'[35] Hudson and Maria were affectionate and adoring with one another throughout their marriage. When they were separated because of ministry they wrote constant letters to one another, full of tender, loving words—Hudson even encoded some of his letters to maintain privacy when expressing his tenderest thoughts. Her death was a great blow to him, but God would see him through it, and in retrospect, had prepared him for it.

The year before this 'hardest year', Hudson Taylor had an awakening to what it means to be united to Christ. This is not to say that prior to this he had no sense or knowledge of his union with Jesus. Rather, in 1869 it suddenly became very real and clear to him. 'When my agony of soul was at its height...the Spirit of God revealed to me the truth of our oneness with Jesus as I had never known it before.'[36] Hudson's close friend recounted this realisation:

> He walked up and down the room saying, 'Oh Mr Judd, God has made me a new man! God has made me a new man! I see that I *am* a branch in Christ, really united to Him; I have not to *make* myself a branch [John 15:5]. If I have a thousand dollars in the Bank and ask the clerk at the counter to give me five hundred, putting out my hand to receive them, he cannot refuse them to my hand and say 'They are Mr Taylor's'; for my hand is part of myself...I am part of

---

35 Ibid., p. 264.
36 Piper, p. 97.

Christ, and what is His I can take.' His faith had now taken hold of the fact of his union—living and actual union—with Christ.[37]

This sudden increase in realisation of what it meant to be united to Jesus had a huge effect on Hudson Taylor's life and ministry. One outcome was the way it helped him through immense pain and suffering. Taylor was beset by deep grief over the many losses and heartaches he faced in his life and grieved deeply. However, he was able to write later in his life, 'In the presence of bereavement, in the deepest sorrows of life, He has drawn so near to me that I have said to myself, "Is it possible that the precious one who is in His presence can have more of the presence of God than I have?"'[38] Others saw it in him too. When he journeyed to Australia to encourage recruits to join CIM in China, a minister who met him wrote, 'Here was a man almost sixty years of age, bearing tremendous burdens, yet absolutely calm and untroubled.'[39]

Another significant burden was to come towards the end of Taylor's life. In 1899, unrest among the people would spill over into a violent uprising that became known as the Boxer Rebellion (after a group involved called the 'Righteous and Harmonious Fists', or simply 'Boxers' by

---

37 Broomhall, *Hudson Taylor & China's Open Century: Book Five: Refiner's Fire*, p. 214.

38 *China's Millions,* No. 110, Vol. IX, August 1884, 102. Cited in Piper, p. 101.

39 Cited in *ibid*, p. 99.

European correspondents). It was an uprising against foreign influence, and sought to destroy foreigners, their property, and Chinese Christians. An imperial decree ordered that all foreigners be killed, and Christianity, viewed as a foreign and therefore dangerous religion, be exterminated.

Europeans, and Chinese people who were deemed too European, were massacred across China. However, there were some incredible exceptions. In one instance, when the edict came through that 'All foreigners are to be killed without fail. If they withdraw (to the coast) they are none the less to be killed', two officials in a local telegram office took it upon themselves to make some minor, but life-saving changes. They swapped the two occurrences of the word 'kill' for the word 'protect'. The edict therefore went forth in their province, 'All foreigners are to be protected without fail. If they withdraw (to the coast) they are none the less certainly to be protected.' For this, the two officials were seized and tortured to death in the cruellest manner. The missionaries who survived because of these officials' intervention called the event 'inexplicable' and 'marvellous.'[40]

The uprising lasted until September 1901. In that time, 135 missionaries and 53 of their children were massacred. Some 79 CIM missionaries were killed (58

---

40 The account of this episode is found in Archibald E. Glover, *A Thousand Miles of Miracle in China: A Personal Record of God's Delivering Power from the Hands of the Imperial Boxers* (Chicago, IL: Moody Press, 1959), pp. 316-7.

adults, 21 children), accounting for nearly half of all deaths among gospel workers during this period. Taylor, who was ill in Switzerland when these tragedies unfolded, never completely recovered from the shock and grief. Writing to CIM in Shanghai, he wrote, 'It is a wonderful honour He has put on us as a Mission to be trusted with so great a trial, and to have among us so many counted worthy of a martyr's crown. Some who have been spared have perhaps suffered more than some of those taken, and our Lord will not forget.'[41] He retired as the general director of CIM the year after in 1902, and died back in China in 1905. Amazingly, particularly to the Chinese, he refused to accept compensation for the loss of life and property in the rebellion, which led to Chinese people issuing declarations that applauded Christians for their forgiving and generous spirit.

Taylor's Legacy

Hudson Taylor, by God's grace, was able to make an incredible impact on China with the good news of Jesus in his lifetime, and left a legacy that remains long after his death. His nightmares over the millions in China dying without God led to a Christian witness throughout China that persists until today, in spite of the difficulties followers of Jesus faced then and now for their faith. How was Taylor able to make such an impact in this place? Taylor's own words encourage us to keep looking

---

41 Taylor and Taylor, *Biography of James Hudson Taylor*, p. 498.

to Jesus as we seek to bear fruit in our own lives, and through us, in the lives of others:

> An easy, non-self-denying life will never be one of power. Fruit bearing involves cross-bearing. There are not two Christs—an easy-going one for easy-going Christians, and a suffering, toiling one for exceptional believers. There is only one Christ. Are you willing to abide in *him*, and thus to bear much fruit?[42]

For further reading

Piper, John, *A Camaraderie of Confidence: The Fruit of Unfailing Faith in the Lives of Charles Spurgeon, George Muller, and Hudson Taylor* (Wheaton, IL: Crossway, 2016).

Taylor, J. Hudson, *Hudson Taylor: The Autobiography of a Man Who Brought the Gospel to China* (Minneapolis, MN: Bethany House Publishers, 1987).

For the adventurous

Taylor, Dr and Mrs Howard, *Biography of James Hudson Taylor* (London: Hodder and Stoughton, 1973).

Taylor, Howard and Howard Mrs Taylor, *Hudson Taylor's Spiritual Secret* (London: China Inland Mission, 1935).

---

42 Taylor and Taylor, *Hudson Taylor's Spiritual Secret*, p. 202.

Charles Spurgeon Preaching, Prayer and Perseverance

Stuart Coulton

Larger than life

On Sunday evening, September 20, 1874 Charles Haddon Spurgeon rose to preach at the Metropolitan Tabernacle on the topic of the sinfulness of little sins. After he had completed his sermon he invited a visiting American preacher—Dr George Pentecost—to speak from the platform. Pentecost took the opportunity to add to Spurgeon's sermon by inveighing against the evils of tobacco smoking, cigars in particular. Spurgeon was well known to his large congregation as a man who enjoyed cigars, and it was with some anticipation that the congregation waited as Spurgeon rose to thank the visiting preacher. The *Daily Telegraph* newspaper reported that Spurgeon spoke with some humour as he thanked Dr Pentecost, told the congregation that he did not consider smoking to be a sin and concluded that he hoped, by the grace of God, to now go home and enjoy smoking a cigar to the glory of God![1]

C.H. Spurgeon was never a man to shy away from controversy.

In March 1892, less than two months after his death, a short obituary for Spurgeon appeared in *The English Illustrated Magazine*. It was written by a Dr H.R. Haweis who told the story of his friend who had commented to Spurgeon that many thought him conceited. Spurgeon's reply, said with a smile, was:

> Do you see these bookshelves? They contain hundreds, nay thousands of my sermons translated into every language under heaven. Well now, add to this that ever since I was twelve years old there never has been built a place large enough to hold the numbers of people who wished to hear me preach, and, upon my honour, when I think of it, I wonder I am not more conceited than I am.[2]

Though there was at times something disarming about his honesty, certainly Spurgeon recognised that his chief

---

1   *Daily Telegraph*, September 23, 1874. See also, *Isle of Ely Gazette* (*Cambridgeshire Times*), October 3, 1874.

2   *The English Illustrated Magazine*, March 1892. Vol. 9 (1891/1892). https://babel.hathitrust.org/cgi/pt?id=mdp.39015056059630;view=1up;seq=515;skin=mobile The reference to Spurgeon's age was either an exaggeration or a misprint. He was not even converted at twelve! See Lewis A. Drummond, *Spurgeon: Prince of Preachers* (Grand Rapids, MI: Kregel, 1992), p. 258. Also, W.Y. Fullerton, *C. H. Spurgeon: A Biography* (London: Williams & Norgate, 1920), p. 87. Fullerton substitutes 'twenty' for 'twelve'.

struggle was with pride. As early as 1855 he wrote to his soon-to-be wife, Susannah, of his 'sad decline in spiritual things', which he attributed mainly to the early success of his ministry—'I tremble at the giddy height on which I stand'.[3]

More than most, perhaps, Spurgeon had reason to be watchful.

His name has been synonymous with preaching since he first mounted a pulpit as a teenager. By the time Spurgeon finished his long ministry in London, over 2,000 of his sermons had been published; more than 14,500 new members had been added by baptism to his congregation since his arrival (many of them were new converts, though not all remained at the church); and he was a national figure serving a church of 6,000 members. On October 7, 1857 at Crystal Palace he preached to his largest audience—over 23,600 people at a National Day of Prayer and Fasting.

Spurgeon was nothing to look at. Short—around 5 feet, 6 inches—and thickset with a big head, protruding teeth and a round boyish face. But he had a sense of theatre that he never lost, though he toned it down a little as he grew older. He would sometimes pull out a bright handkerchief, often polka dot, and wave it

---

3   Charles H. Spurgeon, *Autobiography*, vol. 1, *The Early Years, 1834–1859*, rev. ed. (Edinburgh: The Banner of Truth, 1962), p. 299.

about as he spoke.[4] And he was innovative for his day. Using catchy sermon titles ('*Turn or Burn*'[5]) and colourful posters plastered around London, his sermons were often constructed around something that would both reflect the text and grab the attention.

We might be tempted to call him showy, lacking the substance of solid (or perhaps that is stolid) preaching. However, for Spurgeon being relevant, interesting and newsworthy were not sins. He believed in simple words that possessed fire. In fact he once accused preachers who aimed to reach a few 'intellectuals' in the congregation of leading their congregation to break the fourth commandment, because the majority of their hearers had to labour so hard on the Sabbath to understand them as they preached! His suggestion was the formation of a Lord's Day Rest Society! What people needed to hear, Spurgeon insisted, was the simple gospel—to hear of Jesus.[6]

Although he was first and foremost an evangelical, Spurgeon was also a Baptist by strong conviction. He said in 1855 at the annual session of the London

---

4   Lewis A. Drummond, *Spurgeon: Prince of Preachers* (Grand Rapids, MI: Kregel, 1992), p. 195.

5   This was the title of Spurgeon's sermon on Psalm 7:12 preached on December 7, 1856. See Charles H. Spurgeon, *Metropolitan Tabernacle Pulpit: Sermons* (London: Passmore & Alabaster, 1856).

6   Spurgeon, 'The Glory of our Strength: A Sermon Published on Thursday, April 15, 1909, Delivered on Thursday Evening, February 13, 1873,' in Charles H. Spurgeon, *Metropolitan Tabernacle Pulpit: Sermons* (London: Passmore & Alabaster, 1909).

Baptists that the Baptists were the 'elect of the elect!'[7] He had strong views about the truth of adult baptism, criticising evangelicals who belonged to the Church of England (he thought the Church of England should be disestablished, i.e. legally separated from the State) for belonging to an institution that Spurgeon argued taught baptismal regeneration.[8] At the height of the controversy he had a birdbath installed in his front yard—made from a baptismal font![9]

When he died on January 31, 1892 memorial services were held for him—at 11 a.m., 3 p.m., 7 p.m. and again at 10.30 p.m., which began half an hour early because the building was already packed. In all, 20,000 people attended on the day.[10]

Conversion

Spurgeon was born in Essex in 1834 into a family of strong Christian nonconformist convictions. Nonconformists refused to become members of the Church of England, insisting instead on their freedom to worship outside the established church in 'independent' churches like the Baptists. Socially this meant that they were disadvantaged in many respects. It was late in the

---

7   Drummond, *Spurgeon*, p. 207.

8   Tom Nettles, *Living by Revealed Truth: The Life and Pastoral Theology of Charles Haddon Spurgeon* (Fearn, Scotland: Christian Focus, 2013), pp. 513–7.

9   Drummond, *Spurgeon*, p. 486.

10 Ibid., p. 754.

nineteenth century before a nonconformist could take a degree from Oxford or Cambridge. They were regarded with suspicion and at times scorned by members of the Church of England. But Spurgeon's family exposed him from an early age to the writings of the English Puritans— who aroused guilt and a strong sense of sinfulness in the young Spurgeon:

> ... [T]he Great Husbandman came and began to plough my soul. Ten black horses were His team [the 10 commandments] ... and the justice of God, like a ploughshare, tore my spirit. I was condemned, undone, destroyed,—lost, helpless, hopeless,—I thought hell was before me.[11]

Despite his exposure to the Puritans all that he had was a strong sense of wanting something he could do to make his soul right with God. 'Oh the many times that I wished the preacher would tell me something to do that I might be saved! ... If he had said 'take off your shoes ... and run to John o 'Groat's' I would not even have gone home first'.[12]

It was on January 6, 1850 that Spurgeon found himself in a snowstorm whilst walking to the church he planned to attend. Unable to continue he turned aside to a small Primitive Methodist church. The minister failed to arrive, snowed in by the storm, so finally a man got

11 Spurgeon, *Autobiography,* 1:53.
12 Ibid., 1:69.

up to preach. Spurgeon's description was that he really was quite 'stupid', having no choice than to stay with the text—'*Look unto me and be ye saved, all the ends of the earth'*—as he had nothing else to say! He repeated the verse with brief simple comments for ten minutes or so before fixing his eye upon Spurgeon with the words: 'Young man, you look very miserable ... and you always will be miserable ... in life ... and in death—if you don't obey my text ... look to Jesus ...' [13] Spurgeon said he was '... possessed with that one thought ... the darkness had rolled away ...' [14]

Ministry

Spurgeon was fifteen years old at the time he was converted and only a few years later, having preached once at a very small church in Waterbeach [near Cambridge], he was asked, that as they were struggling to find a minister, if he would continue to preach regularly there. He was still only seventeen! Spurgeon had no formal theological training and in fact never undertook such studies. At one stage Spurgeon looked into the possibility of study, but through an odd misunderstanding he missed the chance. On one occasion, Spurgeon had arranged to discuss the opportunity to study at Stepney College (a Baptist training College) with the Tutor, Dr Angus. However, they proceeded to wait for

13 Ibid., 1:87–8.
14 Ibid., 1:88.

one another in different rooms, and subsequently missed meeting altogether![15] That was as close as Spurgeon came to theological study. He did, however, possess an astonishing volume of learning through his own reading, especially of Puritans like John Bunyan and Richard Sibbes.[16]

He preached to such effect at Waterbeach that he was invited to preach and eventually become pastor of the New Park Street Baptist church in London in 1854, a few months short of his twentieth birthday. It was a congregation with a noble history for the previous 200 years, but had fallen on lean times. Spurgeon had an almost immediate impact—though critics abounded, especially in the Press.

> Mr Spurgeon preaches himself. He is nothing unless he is an actor … exhibiting … matchless impudence … indulging in coarse familiarity with holy things … ranting and colloquial … strutting up and down the platform … and boasting of his own intimacy with heaven with nauseating frequency.[17]

Even a friend called him 'the sauciest dog that ever barked in a pulpit.'[18]

---

15 Ibid., 1:207.

16 Drummond, *Spurgeon*, p. 572.

17 *The Sheffield & Rotherham Independent*, April 28, 1855. Cited in Spurgeon, *Autobiography*, 1:321.

18 W.Y. Fullerton, *C. H. Spurgeon: A Biography* (London: Williams & Norgate, 1920), p. 51.

Perhaps that helps explain him—Spurgeon as a young man was at times arrogant, loose with his language. Even as he grew older he never lost that sharp edge which marked him out as being different, and which drew people to hear him. He spoke and acted without accommodation to suit respectability. He was frank and blunt on most topics. He certainly polarised people. Bishop Wilberforce, son of the anti-slavery campaigner William Wilberforce, was asked once whether he wished that the Anglicans had someone like Spurgeon. His reply was that 'Thou shalt not covet thy neighbour's ass'.[19] As Spurgeon's popularity grew, so eventually the criticism abated, though it never ceased entirely.

In the midst of soaring congregational numbers and enormous public recognition came tragedy. In 1856 the decision was made to build a much larger church auditorium to accommodate the growing congregation. At this point the church voted to change its name to the Metropolitan Tabernacle—recognition that Spurgeon's ministry was to all of London.[20] Whilst waiting for a larger building to be built, the congregation moved to the Surrey Gardens Music Hall—a large venue seating 10,000 people and regarded as a bold and even controversial move. A secular amusement hall being used for sacred worship! Many in the wider community were highly critical of the move. On Sunday October 19,

---

19 Fullerton, *Spurgeon*, p. 116.

20 *Charles H. Spurgeon* (www.wholesomewords.org/biography/biospurgeon6.html)

1856, the first service was conducted with an estimated 10,000 people squeezed into the Hall and another 10,000 said to be outside. Part way through the service the cry of 'Fire' echoed around the vast chamber and others yelled that the galleries were collapsing. It was believed by some eyewitnesses to have been a planned attempt to disrupt the service. In the ensuing panic Spurgeon called for calm, tried to preach but couldn't for the chaos. A hymn was sung and Spurgeon dismissed the crowd. Unknown to Spurgeon, seven people were trampled to death in the stampede and twenty-eight worshippers were taken to hospital.[21]

When Spurgeon was told what had happened he fell into a deep depression. He felt responsible for the deaths. He wrote in his first book *The Saint and his Saviour*:

> ... who can conceive the anguish of my sad spirit? I refused to be comforted; tears were my meat by day, and dreams my terror by night. I felt as I had never done before ... prayer yielded no balm to me ...[22]

The Press pilloried Spurgeon over the tragedy. They accused him of not caring about those killed, seeking to simply make money, preaching 'vile blasphemies' as the

---

21 Spurgeon, *Autobiograhy*, 1:431–6.

22 Spurgeon, *The Saint and His Saviour: The Progress of the Soul in the Knowledge of Jesus* (London: Hodder & Stoughton, 1880), pp. 371–2.

dead were carried out![23] One paper used the tragedy to accuse Spurgeon of 'degrading the pulpit to a far lower level than that of the broadest buffoonery of the stage' before going on to a discussion of crowd behaviour and the construction of public buildings![24]

Spurgeon was absolved of any responsibility for the deaths, but the depression was to plague him throughout his life. Spurgeon's biographer, Lewis Drummond, says that the event left him with a struggle against physical illness for the remainder of his life.[25] William Williams, who had been a student at the Pastor's College and a good friend to Spurgeon over many years, believed that his 'comparatively early death might be in some measure due to the furnace of mental suffering he endured on and after that fearful night'.[26]

The work of the congregation continued to grow despite the frailty of its pastor. Its membership stood at 313 in 1854, and grew exponentially to reach nearly 1,500 by 1860. From 1861–1870 the numbers grew to over 4,000 and by 1881 it was the largest evangelical church in the world with well over 5,000 members. Most Sundays the building was full at both morning and evening services. Remarkably, most growth

---

23 Spurgeon, *Autobiography*, 1:438–42.

24 *The Illustrated London News*, October 25, 1856.

25 Drummond, *Spurgeon*, p. 245.

26 W. Williams, *Personal Reminiscences of Charles Haddon Spurgeon* (London: The Religious Tract Society, 1895), p. 46.

was through conversion rather than transfer.[27] Between 1863 and 1866, 80 per cent of those who joined the church were by 'conversion and baptism.'[28] Even if some were first time Baptists from other churches, the numbers still suggest a high conversion rate. This was always Spurgeon's passion.

This remarkable success of the Tabernacle thrust Spurgeon into the public sphere. Spurgeon was not one to back down on matters he believed to be important. We have touched briefly on his part in the controversy over baptismal regeneration. Of far greater pain to Spurgeon was what he termed the Down-Grade controversy. The controversy arose out of Spurgeon's implacable opposition to the growing tide of theological liberalism sweeping through England in the latter half of the nineteenth century. Theological liberalism cast doubt upon Scripture and consequently many of the key doctrines of the Christian faith. As such it posed a threat to orthodox Christian faith.

For Spurgeon the issue at the heart of the controversy was that of the authority of the Bible. There were voices within the Baptist Union which were casting doubt on the truth of Scripture, and with that came an increasing scepticism about the virgin birth, the divinity of Jesus, His atoning death and resurrection:

---

27 Arnold Dallimore, *Spurgeon: A New Biography* (Edinburgh: Banner of Truth, 1988), p. 83.

28 Drummond, *Spurgeon*, p. 285.

A new religion has been initiated, which is no more Christianity than chalk is cheese; and this religion, being destitute of moral honesty, palms itself off as the old faith with slight improvements, and on this plea usurps pulpits which were erected for gospel preaching. The Atonement is scouted, the inspiration of Scripture is derided, the Holy Spirit is degraded into an influence, the punishment of sin is turned into fiction, and the resurrection into a myth, and yet these enemies of our faith expect us to call them brethren...[29]

Spurgeon identified what he considered to be an inevitable consequence of this teaching, and evidence of its lack of truth, in the spiritual decline of congregations associated with it.

At the back of doctrinal falsehood comes a natural decline of spiritual life ... [a]re churches in a right condition when they have only one meeting for prayer in a week, and that a mere skeleton? ... Are there few conversions? Do the congregations dwindle? Who wonders that this is the case when the spirit of prayer has departed?[30]

On October 28, 1887 Spurgeon withdrew from the Baptist Union. The Council of the Baptist Union responded by censuring Spurgeon. The breach in fellowship was a painful one for Spurgeon, particularly so when he

---

29 Spurgeon, 'Another Word Concerning the Downgrade,' *Sword & Trowel* (August 1887).

30 Ibid.

learned that the 'evil leaven' (as Spurgeon called this liberal theology) had infected even some graduates of the Pastor's College he had founded. For Spurgeon this was the 'sorest wound of all'.[31]

Whilst Spurgeon is best known for his preaching and that was his great focus, preaching was not the sum total of his vocation as a pastor. He had a deep desire to see souls saved, a love for Christian unity (though not at any cost) and a pastoral heart. During the cholera plague of 1855 he immersed himself in visitation to his sick and sometimes dying congregation. 'I do not know how to keep from constant weeping ... when I see others die', he wrote to his father.[32]

Spurgeon's England was that of Dickens, and Spurgeon preached against the vice and corruption of his day as well as the social inequities. He was not a radical in this area, in that he did not advocate the end of class or social distinctions, and certainly was not a socialist. However, Spurgeon did believe in justice. Thus in the magazine he founded and named 'Sword and Trowel' he wrote:

Schemes and plans are all very well, but he who waits till a scheme has put a chicken in his pot will go without a pullet for a lifetime ... We cannot be content to be pampered while our brethren pine in want. Down with the barriers and let the rich and poor meet together, for the Lord is the Maker of them all.[33]

---

31 *Sword & Trowel* (March 1888).

32 Drummond, *Spurgeon*, p. 221.

33 Quoted in Drummond, *Spurgeon*, p. 401.

He didn't simply talk but he did something about it. The Stockwell Orphanages began in 1867 (with a boys' home) and 1879 (a girls' home). Hundreds of children were cared for within an explicitly Christian environment, and along with the Pastors' College for the training of future church leaders occupied a significant portion of Spurgeon's time. In addition a Ladies Benevolent Society was formed to supply clothing to the poor and another to care for poor women who were pregnant, and even one to provide clothing for poor clergy!

Spurgeon struggled with depression most of his life. In addition to his role as pastor of the Metropolitan Tabernacle, Spurgeon taught students as they prepared for vocational ministry. He devoted one of his lectures to what he styled 'The Minister's Fainting Fits'—in other words, depression. Reflecting on his own trials, he wrote:

> Knowing by most painful experience what deep depression of spirit means, being visited therewith at seasons by no means few or far between, I thought it might be consolatory to some … if I gave my thoughts thereon, that younger men might not fancy that some strange thing had happened to them when they became for a season possessed by melancholy.[34]

He identified that physical causes may be involved (he suffered severe gout which meant his arms and legs

---

34 Spurgeon, *Lectures to My Students: Complete and Unabridged*, new ed. (Grand Rapids, MI: Zondervan, 1954), p. 154.

were often badly swollen), as also might mental illness, posing the question to his students: *is any man altogether sane?*[35] He goes on to identify some particular reasons why pastors may suffer depression, including the weight of people's souls: *It is our duty and privilege to exhaust our lives for Jesus;*[36] leading a congregation is lonely work; and the lack of proper rest: *Rest time is not waste time ... in the long run we shall do more by sometimes doing less.*[37] For Spurgeon it was summed up in the striking phrase—'brain-weariness'.[38]

Spurgeon's constant suffering, physical, mental or spiritual, prompted him to turn to the Cross. It was at the Cross that Spurgeon could see that God was sovereign over suffering, and at the Cross that he could know that God had experienced suffering through His own Son.[39] For Spurgeon, suffering was the context out of which God does good in and through His people. It was the *best piece of furniture I have in my house.*[40]

---

35 Spurgeon, *Lectures*, p. 155.

36 Ibid., pp. 156-7.

37 Ibid., pp. 160-1.

38 'Letter from Mr Spurgeon' 1 March, 1885 in C. H. Spurgeon, *Metropolitan Tabernacle Pulpit: Sermons* (London: Passmore & Alabaster, 1885).

39 P.J. Morden, *Communion with Christ and His People: The Spirituality of C.H. Spurgeon* (Eugene, OR: Pickwick Publications, 2013), p. 265.

40 Spurgeon, 'The Pity of the Lord—The Comfort of the Afflicted' in Spurgeon, *The Metropolitan Tabernacle Pulpit: Sermons* (London: Passmore & Alabaster, 1845).

Spurgeon's Legacy

Whilst Spurgeon is often described as the 'Prince' of Preachers, it is important to also recognise where he located the source of the power of his preaching: in prayer. Amidst all the activity—sermons and theological college, theological controversies and orphanages—Spurgeon was a man of prayer. When asked once why he was so successful he simply replied, 'My people pray for me.'[41] Indeed Spurgeon acknowledged that when he came to the New Park Street Chapel he had 'the privilege of ministering from the first to a praying people.'[42] It was in their prayers that Spurgeon located the key to the remarkable impact of his preaching ministry.

Firstly, Spurgeon understood that prayer was driven by the impact of grace in a person's life. Prayer for Spurgeon was an awesome privilege and an onerous responsibility laid upon the people of God. It was not a trifle, and certainly not to be taken for granted nor treated lightly. The believer could pray with confidence because the grace of God in the Lord Jesus Christ makes prayer possible. So our weak faith and our sin-smeared lives, our faulty words and our worries and doubts—none prevent us from praying because we come to a throne of grace

---

41 Dallimore, *Spurgeon*, 49. See also Spurgeon's sermon on 2 Corinthians 1:11 in C.H. Spurgeon, *Only a Prayer-Meeting* (Fearn, Scotland: Christian Focus, 2000), p. 139.

42 Spurgeon, *Autobiography*, 1:263.

where Jesus speaks on our behalf.[43] Spurgeon was quick to insist that the prayers of the ordinary believer needed simply to come from a heart that desired God and His glory—everything else was secondary. As Spurgeon expressed it with his customary flair:

> The prayer which mounts to heaven may have but very few of the tail feathers of adornment about it, but it must have the strong wing feathers of intense desire! ...It must not be as the peacock, gorgeous for beauty, but it must be as the eagle, for soaring aloft ... Verbiage is generally nothing better in prayer than a miserable fig leaf with which to cover the nakedness of an unawakened soul.[44]

Whilst acknowledging that he felt 'more dissatisfied with my prayers than with anything else I do',[45] Spurgeon's sermons are full of practical ideas for prayer along with encouragements to persevere in this work of grace, even when the results are not encouraging:

> In beginning to pray, dear friends, you feel as if you did not pray. The groanings of your spirit, when you rise from your knees are such that you think there is nothing in them. What a blotted, blurred, smeared prayer it is. Never mind; you are not come to the

---

43 See for example Spurgeon's sermon on Hebrews 4:16 preached on November 19, 1871 in C. H. Spurgeon, *Metropolitan Tabernacle Pulpit: Sermons* (London: Passmore & Alabaster, 1871).

44 C. H. Spurgeon, *Metropolitan Tabernacle Pulpit: Sermons* (London: Passmore & Alabaster, 1869).

45 Spurgeon, *Metropolitan Tabernacle Pulpit* (1871).

throne of justice … your broken words, your gaspings, and stammerings are before a throne of grace.[46]

Prayer was a response of the heart as well as the mind to God's grace:

Time spent in quiet prostration of soul before the Lord is most invigorating … Quiet contemplation, still worship, unuttered rapture … Brethren, rob not your heart of the deep sea joys.…[47]

Ours is a Christian culture deeply imbued with rationalism. We can be suspicious of those who use the language of Spurgeon to speak of our relationship with God. It is harder to define, easier to abuse, difficult to account for entirely in rational and easily replicated terms. But time to reflect on what God is doing in our lives; to *be still and know that I am God* (Psalm 46:10), and to worship are surely necessities for all believers. We may perhaps be rebuked by Spurgeon that not only do we rob ourselves of the deep seas of such joy—we often don't even want them!

This passionate, warm-hearted devotion was evident when Spurgeon preached on prayer. In a sermon on Psalm 70:5 Spurgeon dismissed formalised prayers that displayed little emotion or depth of concern. For Spurgeon prayer was wrestling with God:

---

46 Ibid.
47 Spurgeon, *Lectures*, p. 51.

> Mere prayer sayers, who do not pray at all, forget to argue with God; … Do not reckon you have prayed unless you have pleaded, for pleading is the very marrow of prayer.[48]

Not that Spurgeon believed God needed to be pestered or harangued into giving answers to prayer! However, the attitude of the one who prays was important to Spurgeon. A pleading heart indicated an approach to God that was serious and sincere, not careless and disengaged.

Secondly, prayer for Spurgeon was the foundation for all effective Christian ministry. Without the work of God, no ministry, program or sermon could have a lasting impact. It was God who had to undertake spiritual regeneration. Therefore prayer was essential. In a sermon he preached in 1862 Spurgeon insisted that:

> … we cannot glorify Christ without the indwelling of the Holy Ghost. We may pant, and long, and pray that we may have helped to honour our Master, but we shall only dishonour him and disgrace his cause, unless the Holy Spirit hold us up and strengthen us.

He went on to say that the programs of the church were dead without prayer and the Holy Spirit who comes in answer to our prayers:

> Oh, without prayer what are the Church's agencies, but the stretching out of a dead man's arm, or the

48 Spurgeon, *Metropolitan Tabernacle Pulpit* (1871).

lifting up of the lid of a blind man's eye? Only when the Holy Spirit comes, is there any life and force and power.[49]

It is this conviction that the work of the Church—preaching and pastoring, loving, evangelising and proclaiming—was firstly God's work, that drove Spurgeon's dependence upon prayer. How can anyone be raised from death to life? Only when God the author of life breathes life into them. How will God breathe new life into someone? By His Holy Spirit. When will God send His Spirit? When the people of God pray.

> The one thing then which we want, is the Spirit of God. Do not say that we want money; we shall have it soon enough when the Spirit touches men's hearts. Do not say that we want buildings, churches, edifices; all these may be very well in subserviency, but the main want of the Church is the Spirit, and men into whom the Spirit may be poured. If there were only one prayer which I might pray before I died, it should be this; 'Lord, send thy Church men filled with the Holy Ghost, and with fire.'[50]

Such intercessory prayer—for ourselves and for others—sets prayer at the heart of the Christian experience. Spurgeon rejoiced in a congregation of prayerful men and women; he recognised the utter dependence of his

49   Ibid. (1862).
50   Ibid. (1864).

ministry on their prayers and his own; and clearly saw that for Christ's kingdom to flourish in any age, there must be both a bold proclamation of God's Word along with a bold intercession for the work of that Word.

> Never account prayer second to preaching. No doubt prayer in the Christian church is as precious as the utterance of the gospel. To speak to God for men is a part of the Christian priesthood that should never be despised.[51]

In lecturing the students in the Pastor's College he founded, Spurgeon warned them that as those called by God to preach they had firstly the same responsibility to pray held by all believers—lest they be hypocritical. But their prayers as leaders of God's people had to exceed those of others, otherwise they were disqualifying themselves from their position as leaders within the people of God.[52]

> ... if you become lax in secret devotion, not only will you need to be pitied, but your people also; and, in addition to that, you will be blamed ...[53]

Thirdly, Spurgeon set prayer within the community of God's people. At the Metropolitan Tabernacle services were held twice on Sunday and again on Thursday

---

51 Ibid. (1871).

52 Spurgeon, *Lectures*, p. 42.

53 Ibid., p. 43.

evening. Prayer was not an incidental part of these services but, along with the sermon, a central feature. So Spurgeon was loathe to give up the main prayer of the gathering to any visitor, preferring to lead the congregation in prayer himself.[54] Although he declared short public prayers to be the best prayers,[55] his own prayers during Sunday gatherings often ran to over 1,200 words![56] Spurgeon's prayers were rich in biblical imagery and masterpieces of rhetorical skill. D.L. Moody, the great American evangelist, visited the Tabernacle on a number of occasions to hear Spurgeon preach. Moody declared that much as he had been blessed by Spurgeon's preaching, he had been even more impressed by his prayers.[57]

Whilst Spurgeon encouraged members to join in prayer together immediately before public worship,[58] Monday evening was the main prayer service for the church with over one thousand people attending![59]

---

54 Peter J. Morden, *Communion with Christ and His People: The Spirituality of C. H. Spurgeon* (Eugene, OR: Pickwick Publications, 2013), p. 141.

55 Spurgeon, *Metropolitan Tabernacle Pulpit* (1869).

56 See Spurgeon, *The Pastor in Prayer: A Collection of the Sunday Morning Prayers of C.H. Spurgeon* (Edinburgh: Banner of Truth Trust, 2004).

57 Spurgeon, *Autobiography*, vol. 2, *The Full Harvest, 1860–1892*, rev. ed. (Edinburgh: The Banner of Truth Trust, 1973), p. 315.

58 Spurgeon, *Only a Prayer-Meeting*, 142. See also Morden, *Communion*, p. 141.

59 Morden, *Communion*, p. 141.

Spurgeon was consistent in insisting that the effectiveness of his ministry was dependent upon the prayers of his people,[60] hence the priority which he gave to such gatherings.

Dr J.I. Packer said that 'prayer is the measure of the man, spiritually, in a way that nothing else is, so that how we pray is as important a question as we can ever face.'[61] Charles Spurgeon would have agreed, and his life bore testimony to that conviction.

For further reading:

Spurgeon, Charles H., *The Saint and His Saviour: The Progress of the Soul in the Knowledge of Jesus* (London: Hodder & Stoughton, 1880).

Fullerton, W. Y., *C. H. Spurgeon: A Biography* (London: Williams & Norgate, 1920).

For the adventurous:

Spurgeon, Charles H., *Lectures to My Students: Complete & Unabridged.* New Ed. (Grand Rapids, MI: Zondervan, 1954).

Drummond, Lewis A., *Spurgeon: Prince of Preachers* (Grand Rapids, MI: Kregel, 1992).

---

60 Spurgeon, *Only a Prayer-Meeting*, p. 139.

61 J.I. Packer, *My Path of Prayer: Personal Experiences of God*, ed. David Hanes (Worthing: Henry E. Walter, 1981), p. 56. Quoted in D.A. Carson, *A Call to Spiritual Reformation: Priorities from Paul and His Prayers* (Grand Rapids, MI: Baker Book House, 1992), p. 17.

Dietrich Bonhoeffer
The Cost of Discipleship

Ian J. Maddock

The public broadcast was cut off before he could finish speaking. Dietrich Bonhoeffer, a precociously talented twenty-six-year-old Lutheran scholar-pastor, hadn't quite reached the climax of his provocative speech entitled 'The Younger Generation's Altered Concept of Leadership.' Just two days earlier, on 30 January, 1933, Adolf Hitler had become the democratically elected Chancellor of Germany—a dizzying rise to power that left many Germans rejoicing, but still others reeling, horrified and unsure quite how to respond. Bonhoeffer stepped into this highly charged environment and delivered a not-so-subtle critique of anyone who dared to exalt themselves as unrivalled Führer (Leader). Such a person, he warned, will inevitably become an idol and amount to a Verführer (Mis-leader) of the people. Those, he declared, 'who set themselves up as gods mock God.'

Whether or not the sudden silencing of Bonhoeffer's prophetic voice was an early instance of brazen censorship by Joseph Goebbels and the Gestapo, or perhaps (despite insidious appearances) simply a case of Bonhoeffer exceeding his allotted time, it was undoubtedly a sign of things to come. His theological dismantling of the *Führerprinzip* (Führer Concept) that day at the Potsdamerstrasse broadcast house set him on a public collision course with the Nazis and the State sponsored *Reichskirche* (German Christians who had sworn allegiance to Hitler and the Third Reich). It also proved to be an eerie premonition of his own life prematurely cut short.

Preparation

That a Bonhoeffer should find themselves at the centre of public intellectual life was not at all surprising given the family's pedigree and appetite for achievement. Dietrich and his twin sister Sabine were born in Breslau on 4 February 1906, the sixth and seventh of eight children born to Paula and Karl Bonhoeffer. Karl was a high-profile psychiatrist and professor at the University of Berlin, while Paula was a university graduate (somewhat rare for a woman in those times) whose father served as Court Preacher for Kaiser Wilhelm II. Dietrich's siblings included Karl-Friedrich (a professor of Chemistry), Klaus (a lawyer who would eventually be executed following his involvement in the failed July 1944 plot to kill Hitler), and Walter, whose death in 1918 on the Western Front proved to be a foretaste of the profound impact war would have on the Bonhoeffer family.

And yet the idea that a Bonhoeffer would choose, of all things, to become a theologian was surprising. Dietrich's family life was cultured and privileged, but not especially religious; the Church was characterised as a 'petty bourgeois institution.' And so, at the age of fourteen, when Bonhoeffer announced, seemingly out of the blue, that he intended to be a theologian, his decision was met with raised eyebrows. In his father's estimation especially, the talented Dietrich was selling himself short. 'At the time you decided to devote yourself to theology,' he later reflected, 'I sometimes thought to myself that a quiet, uneventful minister's life... would really almost be a pity for you. As far as eventfulness is concerned, I was greatly mistaken.'[1]

For the time being, though, when Bonhoeffer set off to study theology at Tübingen in 1923, there was little to hint at the tumultuous events to come, let alone his own role in the unfolding drama. After transferring to the University of Berlin a year later, remarkably he completed his doctorate in 1927 at the age of twenty-one. His dissertation was entitled *Sanctorum Communio* ('The Communion of Saints') and was described at the time as a 'theological miracle' by no less than the eminent Swiss theologian Karl Barth.

---

1   Cited in Eberhard Bethge, *Dietrich Bonhoeffer: A Biography* (Minneapolis: Fortress, 2000), p. 37.

Despite his privileged background, Bonhoeffer's affinity for the marginalised and oppressed would be a defining feature of his life and ministry. He might have been a newly minted 'professional' theologian, but at his core he was always a 'practical' theologian: theology was best applied, not confined to an ivory tower. And so immediately after graduating Bonhoeffer headed to Barcelona to serve as the assistant pastor of a Lutheran church for German expatriates. His time in Spain in 1928 and 1929 coincided with the Great Depression, and with it his first glimpse of abject poverty. His sermons during this period are notable for the way he implored his congregation (comprised mainly of businessmen and diplomats) to aid—or at the very least acknowledge the existence of—the disadvantaged locals in their midst.

Incurably curious and a lifelong traveller, soon afterwards in 1930 Bonhoeffer found himself in New York, the recipient of a scholarship to study at Union Theological Seminary. His sojourn was formative on a number of fronts. First, he seems to have experienced a personal conversion. He wrote afterwards that while in America, 'something happened, something that has changed and transformed my life to the present day. For the first time I discovered the Bible... I had often preached. I had seen a great deal of the Church, and talked and preached about it—but I had not yet become a Christian... Since then everything has changed.'[2]

---

2   Geffrey B. Kelly and F. Burton Nelson (eds.), *A Testament to Freedom: The Essential Writings of Dietrich Bonhoeffer* (New York:

Second, he more than ever became convinced of the theological bankruptcy of Protestant Liberalism. On one occasion, wanting primarily to defend historic orthodoxy (and perhaps secondarily the honour of a fellow German!), Bonhoeffer reflected that, 'A seminary in which it can come about that a large number of students laugh out loud in a public lecture at the quoting of a passage from Luther's *De servo arbitrio* [*The Bondage of the Will*] on sin and forgiveness because it seems to them to be comic has evidently completely forgotten what Christian theology by its very nature stands for.'[3] And third, Bonhoeffer was able to strike up deep friendships with people he wouldn't naturally encounter back home in Germany, including an African-American theological student named Frank Fisher. Throughout his year in America he was regularly involved in the ministry of the Abyssinian Baptist Church in Harlem. He also observed American-style systemic racism first-hand. It gave him fresh eyes to see the evils of anti-Semitism back home and empathise with the plight of the Jews.

It wasn't long before Bonhoeffer would be in a prime position to act on these new insights. In 1931 he accepted a position as a lecturer in theology in Berlin and was also ordained as a Lutheran pastor. Meanwhile, the political climate was undergoing seismic convulsions. The punitive terms of the Treaty of Versailles that followed

Harper Collins, 1995), p. 424.

3   Dietrich Bonhoeffer, *No Rusty Swords: Letters, Lectures and Notes, 1928-1936* (New York: Harper and Row, 1965), p. 91.

Germany's defeat in World War One, together with the devastating economic impact of the Great Depression, had left the German population desperate for restored honour and prosperity—and particularly vulnerable to the promises of an opportunistic demagogue like Adolf Hitler. Within months of ascending to power, in early 1933 Hitler enacted legislation that gave the Nazis virtually unilateral power. Anti-Semitism became the law of the land. 'The Law for the Restoration of the Civil Service,' also introduced in 1933, included the infamous, so-called 'Aryan Clause.' This measure excluded Jews from positions of authority, not just in government and universities, but also in churches. The Nazi edicts were close to home for Bonhoeffer: one of his close friends, Franz Hildebrandt, was a Lutheran pastor of Jewish descent.

Bonhoeffer's prophetic voice

Bonhoeffer's response was swift, insightful, prophetic and brave. In April 1933 he delivered a lecture entitled 'The Church and the Jewish Question' where he argued that, in precluding Christians of Jewish descent from serving as pastors, the State had overstepped its God-given jurisdiction. The Church, Bonhoeffer argued, was faced with three possible courses of action. First, Christians can 'ask the state whether its actions are legitimate'; in other words, 'it can throw the state back on its responsibilities.' Second, and in addition to the first measure, the Church can 'aid the victims of state action.' The Church 'has an unconditional obligation to the victims of any ordering of society,' including— and here Bonhoeffer embodies the radical scope of the Apostle Paul's injunction in Galatians 6:2—those who 'do not belong to the Christian community.' No one could be in any doubt as to which religious group within German society Bonhoeffer specifically had in mind. And yet as provocative as the breadth of this second course of action might have sounded (some among his audience reportedly stood up and left), Bonhoeffer was only warming up. 'The third possibility,' he declared, 'is not just to bandage the victims under the wheel, but to put a spoke in the wheel itself.'[4] Bonhoeffer, in other words, envisaged a time when circumstances would demand Christians respond with direct political intervention, even to the point of martyrdom.

Alongside prominent figures like the theologian Karl Barth and pastor Martin Niemöller, Bonhoeffer quickly found himself part of a breakaway group of dissenting Christians who refused to bow the knee to Hitler. They were styled the 'Confessing Church,' and in 1934 produced the so-called 'Barmen Declaration.' It defiantly repudiated the Führer Principle, exhorting Christians to maintain their first allegiance to Jesus Christ. It rejected the totalitarian claims of Nazism and the idea that

---

4   Ibid., p. 226.

'the church can turn over the form of her message and ordinances at will or according to some dominant ideological and political convictions,' and called the Church to resist losing its identity by being reduced to a mere organ of the state.[5]

And yet Bonhoeffer intuitively recognised that as noble as the Barmen Declaration's sentiments were, gestures such as these would be futile in preventing the Nazis from attempting to realise their worst ambitions. He clearly foresaw a time when faithful Christians would be called to jam the machinery of the state. He wrote to a Swiss friend Erwin Sutz in April 1934: 'While I'm working with the church opposition with all my might, it's perfectly clear to me that this opposition is only a very temporary transitional phase on the way to an opposition of a very different kind.' Anticipating the trajectory of future events with uncanny accuracy, he continued, 'I believe that all of Christendom should be praying with us for the coming resistance 'to the point of shedding blood' and for the finding of people who can suffer it through.'[6]

These disorienting and stressful times took an understandable toll on Bonhoeffer. For one so attracted to the tenets of pacifism, the temptation to retreat into passive acquiescence must have been strong. Indeed,

5   The Barmen Declaration, translated by F.H. Littell, in The German Phoenix (Garden City, NY: Doubleday, 1960) pp. 186-7.

6   K. Clements (ed.), Dietrich Bonhoeffer Works Edition (Minneapolis: Fortress, 2007), 13:135.

when an opportunity arose in late 1933 for him to pastor two German-speaking congregations in London, Bonhoeffer didn't hesitate. Though nor did his friends hesitate to call him to back—and call him out for being, in effect, absent without leave. 'What is all this about "going away," "the quietness of pastoral work," etc., at a moment when you are just wanted in Germany?' scolded Karl Barth in a letter written one month after Bonhoeffer's departure. In an environment that was becoming increasingly dangerous for those who dared to challenge Hitler, Barth's martial language was apt: 'Now, one can on no account play Elijah under the juniper tree or Jonah under the gourd, but must shoot from both barrels!' Now was the moment to 'attend faithfully and bravely to the machine-gun which you have left behind there.' In response to whatever arguments Bonhoeffer might muster to rationalise his departure, Barth simply asked, 'And the German church? And the German churches?' He went on: 'one simply cannot be weary just now. Still less can one go to England! What in the world would you want to do there?' He urged his friend to 'think of only one thing, that you are a German, that the house of your church is on fire... that you must return to your post by the next ship... But I cannot tell you urgently enough that you belong to Berlin and not to London.'[7]

---

7   Bonhoeffer, *No Rusty Swords*, pp. 234-5.

Barth's letter appears to have cut Bonhoeffer to the heart, but it wasn't until 1935 that he eventually returned to Germany, lured home by an invitation to lead an underground Confessing Church seminary at Finkenwalde. 'Brother Bonhoeffer', as he was known to his students, along with his initial cohort of twenty-three seminarians (including close friend and future biographer Eberhard Bethge) spent their time studying the Bible, praying, singing and serving in close-knit community. This season of his life provided the raw material for one of his most enduring works, *Life Together*. Like in many of his writings, Bonhoeffer offers a vision of the Christian life that at first (and even second!) glance provides a stunning rebuke to any desire we might have to retreat into a privatised faith that lacks tangible accountability. For example, he provocatively argued that it isn't enough to confess our sins to God; instead, we need to confess our 'secret sins' to one another. 'As long as our sin remains hidden,' he observed, 'it gnaws away at us and poisons us. Sin creates detritus in the soul. The serpent must stick its head out of its hole in order for it to be clubbed. When another person hears my sins their danger can finally be taken away.' His insights into the human condition were born out of his rich and varied pastoral experience. 'The root of all sin is pride.' In light of this:

> Confession to another human being breaks this arrogance as nothing else can. The old, prideful

Adam dies a disgraceful death in great agony. Since this humiliation is so painful, we would rather bypass it and think that it is enough to confess to God. But in our degradation we find our portion in the disgrace of Christ, who was not ashamed to stand before the world as a sinner. Confession of sin before another person is an act of discipleship to the cross. By confession we gain freedom from pride of flesh or reason.[8]

The Finkenwalde era was short-lived. In 1937 the Nazis formally outlawed the training of Confessing Church pastors, the seminary was shut down, and many of Bonhoeffer's students were arrested by the Gestapo.

By this point Bonhoeffer was well and truly in the Nazis' cross-hairs. They had long recognised his immense talents and now systematically set about denying him influence. In 1936 he was declared a 'Pacifist and Enemy of the State.' In 1938 he was banned from lecturing at the University of Berlin. In 1940 he was forbidden to speak in public on the grounds that he was subverting the people. Bonhoeffer was so aggrieved at this charge he wrote a letter to the authorities in which he vigorously defended his patriotism, even to the point of concluding with the valediction 'Heil Hitler!' In 1941 his right to publish was revoked.

---

8 Dietrich Bonhoeffer, *Spiritual Care,* trans. Jay Rochelle (Minneapolis: Fortress, 1982), p. 63.

Cheap versus Costly Grace

But before the last of these censures had been imposed, in 1937 Bonhoeffer published arguably his most famous work, *Nachfolge* (in German, this means 'discipleship' or 'following'). Subsequent English translations have rendered the title *The Cost of Discipleship*, no doubt as a way of capturing the union of Bonhoeffer's prophetic ministry and untimely martyrdom. In fact, his long-time friend, George Bell, the Bishop of Chichester, began his foreword to *The Cost of Discipleship* by quoting Bonhoeffer's own words: 'When Christ calls a man, he bids him come and die.'[9]

In a context where many Christians had become complacent and were more than willing to cosy up to political power as a way of enhancing the institutional prestige of the Church, *The Cost of Discipleship* was a challenge to faithfully live out the radical demands of Jesus' Sermon on the Mount, whatever the cost that would inevitably follow. Bonhoeffer famously contrasts two types of grace: true (or 'costly') grace, versus its counterfeit, illegitimate sibling (what he styled 'cheap' grace).

What is cheap grace? 'Cheap grace,' according to Bonhoeffer's definition, 'is the preaching of forgiveness without requiring repentance, baptism without church discipline, communion without confession, absolution

---

9   Dietrich Bonhoeffer, *The Cost of Discipleship* (London: SCM, 2001), p. 44.

without personal confession. Cheap grace is grace without discipleship, grace without the cross, grace without Jesus Christ, living and incarnate.' What does cheap grace look like in practice? It manifests itself in the person who says, 'I can go and sin as much as I like, and rely on this grace to forgive me, for after all the world is justified in principle by grace. I can therefore cling to my bourgeois secular existence, and remain as I was before, but without the added assurance that the grace of God will cover me.'[10]

Not surprisingly, Bonhoeffer considered this distorted grace to be 'the deadly enemy of our Church.' He wrote, 'We are fighting to-day for costly grace... Cheap grace means grace as a doctrine, as principle, as system... The world finds in this church a cheap cover-up for sins, for which it shows no remorse and from which it has even less desire to be set free. Cheap grace is, thus, denial of God's living word, denial of the incarnation of the word of God.' By contrast, costly grace 'is costly because it calls us to follow, and it is grace because it calls us to follow Jesus Christ. It is costly because it costs a man his life, and it is grace because it gives a man the only true life. It is costly because it condemns sin, and grace because it justifies the sinner. Above all, it is costly because it cost God the life of his Son.'[11]

Bonhoeffer was simply insisting that if someone is truly justified (forgiven in God's sight), they won't use

10 Ibid., pp. 4, 10.
11 Ibid., pp. 3, 5.

their new status as a license to indulge old ways of living. While affirming a crucial theological insight of the Reformation—that justification is by grace alone through faith alone—Bonhoeffer reminds his readers, then and now, of a fundamental biblical truth: that there's an organic connection between root and fruit. Christians aren't simply saved by grace *from* sin. We're saved *for* discipleship—costly discipleship. In Bonhoeffer's words: 'so far from dispensing him [the justified Christian] from discipleship, this grace only made him a more earnest disciple.' As a result, 'Those who try to use this grace as a dispensation from following Christ are simply deceiving themselves.'[12]

Fight or flight?

As the prospect of war loomed ever closer, and the realization that the Nazi's anti-Semitic bite was just as malevolent as its bark, Bonhoeffer was faced with the constant choice: fight or flight. The urge to resist was strong. In the wake of *Kristallnacht*—a wave of violent attacks on Jewish homes, synagogues and businesses on 9 November, 1938—Bonhoeffer spoke out against this flagrant anti-Semitism and in the process faced the certain ire of the Nazi regime. Justifying his actions, Bonhoeffer is reported to have said, 'Only those who cry out for the Jews can sing Gregorian chants.' In the Bible he inherited from his brother Walter, he underlined Psalm

---

12 Ibid., pp. 9, 11.

74:8 which reads 'they burned all the meeting places of God in the land,' and wrote beside it '9.11.38.' He also underlined the next verse, adding an exclamation mark: 'We do not see our signs; there is no longer any prophet, and there is none among us who knows how long.'

And yet the urge to flee was always in front of him too. Well-meaning friends in America encouraged him to find refuge in the United States before it was too late. Reinhold Niebuhr, his former professor in New York, arranged a teaching post for him at Union Theological Seminary. Bonhoeffer accepted and left Germany on 2 June, 1939. But before he had even spent a month in America Bonhoeffer knew where he needed to be, and it wasn't on a lecture tour of the American Midwest. This time he needed no letter from Karl Barth to coax him back to Germany. Knowing full well the personal dangers that surely awaited him, on 8 July, 1939 Bonhoeffer boarded the very last passenger ship to make a transatlantic crossing before Hitler's invasion of Poland on 1 September. He wrote to Reinhold Niebuhr:

> I have come to the conclusion that I made a mistake in coming to America. I must live through this difficult period in our national history with the people of Germany. I will have no right to participate in the reconstruction of Christian life in Germany after the war if I do not share the trials of this time with my people... Christians in Germany will have to face the terrible alternative of either willing the defeat of their nation in

order that Christian civilization may survive or willing the victory of their nation and thereby destroying civilization. I know which of these alternatives I must choose but I cannot make that choice from security.[13]

To be a German in wartime—especially a man like Bonhoeffer in his early thirties—meant the very real likelihood of military service. His brother-in-law, Hans von Dohnanyi, secured him a position in the *Abwehr* (the military intelligence agency). Ostensibly Bonhoeffer's role entailed leveraging his extensive ecclesial contacts in the United States, the United Kingdom and Scandinavia in order to gauge the political climate among Germany's enemies. In practice, Bonhoeffer was a double-agent, on one occasion helping thirteen Jews escape into neutral Switzerland in a daring plot known as 'Operation 7.' He was also privy to a plot to assassinate Hitler made by members of the Abwehr desperate to rid Germany of their Führer. In such an environment, knowledge was dangerous: mere awareness of resistance activities was tantamount to complicity. Indeed, even though he doesn't seem to have been actively at the centre of this particular assassination attempt, he willed for it to be successful. Faced with the dilemma of either submitting to the governing authorities and supporting genocide or joining an attempted coup, this pacifist-by-conviction came to the point of writing, 'If we claim to be Christian,

---

13 Kelly and Nelson (eds.), *A Testament to Freedom*, p. 504.

there is no room for expediency. Hitler is anti-Christ. Therefore we must be on with our work and eliminate him.'[14]

In retrospect, the lifespan of these highly fraught underground manoeuvres was always going to be brief. Although the Gestapo initially lacked concrete evidence of Bonhoeffer's activities as a double-agent, they became highly suspicious and had him arrested. Although he had just become engaged to be married to Maria von Wedemeyer, once Bonhoeffer entered Tegel prison on 5 April, 1943 his remaining two years on earth were spent entirely in confinement. He kept himself busy with a daily regime of Bible reading, prayer and singing hymns that he had memorised. Throughout this lonely time he also produced some of his most poignant—and enigmatic—writings. These were later published as *Letters and Papers from Prison.* In them Bonhoeffer reflects deeply on the central place of suffering in Christianity—both God's suffering and ours. 'To be a Christian,' he wrote, 'does not mean to be religious in a particular way, to make something of oneself (a sinner, a penitent, or a saint) on the basis of some method or other, but to be a man—not a type of man, but the man that Christ creates in us. It is not the religious act that makes the Christian, but participation in the sufferings of God in the secular life.' Indeed, Bonhoeffer might have been a committed

---

14 Cited in Franklin H. Littell, 'Church Struggle and the Holocaust' in F.H. Littell and H.G. Locke (eds.), *The German Church Struggle and the Holocaust* (Detriot: Wayne State University Press, 1975), p. 15.

churchman, but having witnessed first-hand the abject capitulation of the German Church under the Nazis, he had very little time for 'religion.' From prison he began to contrast true Christianity (provocatively styled as 'religionless Christianity') which begins with God's self-revelation in Jesus (the 'lord of the religionless') with false religion that begins with our idolatrous efforts to fashion God as a patron of our own agendas.[15]

On 20 July, 1944 an assassination attempt against Hitler narrowly failed: the bomb that had been planted under the conference table at the Führer's East Prussian headquarters (known as the Wolf's Lair) had left his pride and clothing in tatters, but his body intact. It sent the Gestapo into a flurry of activity as they quickly set about finding the culprits. Eventually Bonhoeffer's role as a co-conspirator was exposed and his fate was sealed. In his own mind, he had been reconciled to the prospect of his own death for some time. At a low ebb during his confinement at Tegel he had even contemplated suicide: 'not because of consciousness of guilt but because I am already dead.'[16]

Bonhoeffer's final days and legacy

Bonhoeffer's integrity and authentic Christian witness has left a profound—and continuing—impact on the modern Church. Everyone it seems has wanted to claim him for

---

15   Eberhard Bethge (ed.), *Dietrich Bonhoeffer: Letters and Papers from Prison* (New York: Touchstone, 1971), p. 361.

16   Ibid., p. 35.

their own! There's Bonhoeffer the champion of ecumenical relations, who served as the Youth Secretary of the 1931 World Alliance for Promoting International Friendship through the Churches Conference in Cambridge, England. There's Bonhoeffer the champion of social justice, of whom Martin Luther King, Jr. reportedly said: 'If your opponent has a conscience, then follow Gandhi and non-violence. But if your enemy has no conscience like Hitler, then follow Bonhoeffer.' There's Bonhoeffer the champion of Reformation orthodoxy, who famously criticised mainline American Protestantism for preaching 'about virtually everything' except 'the gospel of Jesus Christ, the cross, sin and forgiveness, death and life.'[17] Without doubt he was a complex figure, whose premature death has added mystique to his rich legacy. And yet in many ways he was also a remarkably uncomplicated figure, a role model of singular commitment to following Jesus, for whom discipleship came at a great cost.

In early 1945 he was transferred to the Buchenwald concentration camp and from there to the extermination camp at Flossenbürg. On 8 April, at the request of the little band of fellow-captives, he had the opportunity to serve as a pastor one last time, preaching from Isaiah 53:5: 'By his wounds we are healed.' After a perfunctory trial later that evening in the camp's laundry room, Bonhoeffer was sentenced to death for high treason. In

---

17 Clifford J. Green (ed.), *Dietrich Bonhoeffer Works* (New York: Fortress, 2008), 10:313.

a symbolic reversal, he was exonerated of these charges exactly fifty years later. Bent on revenge, the order for the executions came directly from Adolf Hitler himself. In a matter of weeks, Hitler would take his own life and the war would be over.

On the grey morning of 9 April, 1945 Dietrich Bonhoeffer, along with six other co-resisters (including Admiral Wilhelm Canaris) was hanged. Just two weeks later the Allies would liberate Flossenbürg. There were only a few witnesses to this macabre scene, one of whom included the prison doctor, H. Fischer-Hullstrüng. Unaware of who Bonhoeffer was at the time, some years later he reflected on how, 'The prisoners... were taken from their cells, and the verdicts of court martial read out to them. Through the half-open door in one room of the huts, I saw Pastor Bonhoeffer, before taking off his prison garb, kneeling on the floor praying fervently to his God. I was most deeply moved by the way this lovable man prayed, so devout and so certain that God heard his prayer.' He went on, 'At the place of execution, he again said a prayer and then climbed the steps to the gallows, brave and composed. His death ensued in a few seconds. In the almost 50 years that I have worked as a doctor, I have hardly ever seen a man die so entirely submissive to the will of God.'[18] Bonhoeffer's

---

18 H. Fischer-Hullstrüng,, 'A Report from Flossenbürg,' in W-D Zimmermann and R.G. Smith (eds.), *I Knew Dietrich Bonhoeffer: Reminiscences by His Friends*; trans. K.G. Smith (New York: Harper and Row, 1966), p. 232.

last recorded words were spoken to a captured British Special Intelligence Service agent, Payne Best: 'this is the end—for me, the beginning of life.'[19]

For further reading

Stephen J. Nichols, *Bonhoeffer on the Christian Life: From the Cross, For the World* (Wheaton, IL: Crossway, 2013).

Eric Metaxas, *Bonhoeffer: Pastor, Martyr, Prophet, Spy* (Nashville, TN: Thomas Nelson, 2010).

For the adventurous

Eberhard Bethge, *Dietrich Bonhoeffer: A Biography* (Minneapolis MN: Augsburg Fortress, 2000).

---

19 Payne Best, *The Venlo Incident* (New York: Hutchinson, 1950), p. 200.

Also Available from Christian Focus Publications...

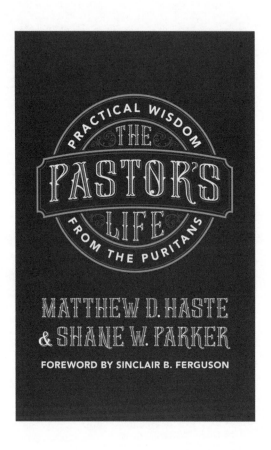

PRACTICAL WISDOM

THE

PASTOR'S

LIFE

FROM THE PURITANS

MATTHEW D. HASTE
& SHANE W. PARKER

FOREWORD BY SINCLAIR B. FERGUSON

ISBN 978-1-5271-0367-2

The Pastor's Life

Practical Wisdom from the Puritans

Matthew D. Haste and Shane W. Parker

The men whose stories appear in this book made up a network of pastors. Through personal contact, or influence, or by reading each other's books, they were bound together in a spiritual brotherhood. They shared a common burden to see God glorified, His Son magnified, and His Spirit honoured by wholesome and practical biblical preaching, wise pastoral counselling, church and family strengthening, and faithful Christian living. Haste and Parker introduce us to these men, their theology, and the lessons we can learn from them.

In this book Matt Haste and Shane Parker have given us the opportunity to gather around the metaphorical table with wise, seasoned pastors, long gone from this visible world. This book can help the reader to think through not just the importance of personal piety and pastoral skill, but also to see examples of how to pursue such things.

Russell D. Moore
President, The Southern Baptist Ethics & Religious Liberty Commission

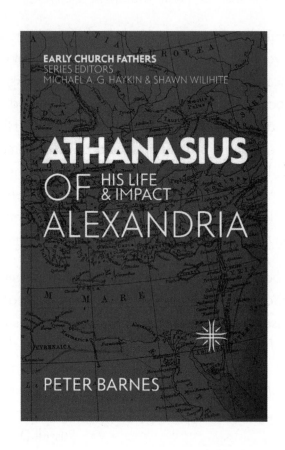

EARLY CHURCH FATHERS
SERIES EDITORS
MICHAEL A. G. HAYKIN & SHAWN WILIHITE

ATHANASIUS

OF HIS LIFE & IMPACT

ALEXANDRIA

PETER BARNES

ISBN 978-1-5271-0392-4

Athanasius of Alexandria

His Life and Impact

Peter Barnes

From the foreword: Until his death in 373, Athanasius was the most formidable opponent of Arianism in the Roman Empire. Ultimately, for him, this fight was not a struggle for ecclesial power or even for the rightness of his theological position. It was a battle for the souls of men and women. Athanasius rightly knew that upon one's view of Christ hung one's eternal destiny. As he wrote to the bishops of Egypt in 356: 'as therefore the struggle that is now set before us concerns all that we are, either to reject or to keep the faith, let us be zealous and resolve to guard what we have received, bearing in mind the confession that was written down at Nicaea.' And by God's grace, his victory in that struggle has been of enormous blessing to the church ever since.

Athanasius, whose name means 'immortal,' lives on in this comprehensive and commendable biography. Barnes shows how the animated controversialist managed a full life, as a Nicene theologian, Alexandrian bishop, and five-time refugee. The influence of the patriarch persists through these informed pages.

Paul Hartog
Professor of Theology, Faith Baptist Theological Seminary,
Ankeny, Iowa

Christian Focus Publications

Our mission statement —

STAYING FAITHFUL

In dependence upon God we seek to impact the world
through literature faithful to His infallible Word, the Bible.
Our aim is to ensure that the Lord Jesus Christ is presented as
the only hope to obtain forgiveness of sin, live a useful life and
look forward to heaven with Him.

Our books are published in four imprints:

CHRISTIAN
FOCUS

Popular works including biographies, commentaries, basic doctrine
and Christian living.

CHRISTIAN
HERITAGE

Books representing some of the
best material from the rich heritage
of the church.

MENTOR

Books written at a level suitable
for Bible College and seminary
students, pastors, and other serious readers. The imprint includes
commentaries, doctrinal studies,
examination of current issues and
church history.

CF4•K

Children's books for quality Bible
teaching and for all age groups: Sunday
school curriculum, puzzle and activity
books; personal and family devotional
titles, biographies and inspirational stories — because you are never too young
to know Jesus!

Christian Focus Publications Ltd,
Geanies House, Fearn, Ross-shire,
IV20 1TW, Scotland, United Kingdom.
www.christianfocus.com